The Silent Sound of Needles

Michael Zwerin

THE SILENT SOUND OF NEEDLES

Prentice-Hall, Inc., Englewood Cliffs, N.J.

13-810234-1

Library of Congress Catalog Card Number: 69-14474

Printed in the United States of America

T

Prentice-Hall International, Inc., London
Prentice-Hall of Australia, Pty. Ltd., Sydney
Prentice-Hall of Canada, Ltd., Toronto
Prentice-Hall of India Private Ltd., New Delhi
Prentice-Hall of Japan, Inc., Tokyo

"Three Crises in the Lives of Dope Fiends," by Wallace White, reprinted by permission of *Esquire*.

To every Joe Sploe who would rather not be putting a needle in his arm, and to all the inactive dope fiends in the house on 123rd Street.

Table of Contents

Part One

THE STREET

1
Freedom

Flagg has fallen off bandstands, vomited backstage, boosted from hotel rooms and nodded out on busses in every state of this Union, plus three Latin-American countries. Late to work —which was often—he would just say, "I got hung up, man." That explained it, as far as he was concerned. An excusable error. "Oh, you got hung up," the bandleader was supposed to say. "I see. You got hung up. That's groovy, man. I understand."

Flagg just came from Lexington, Kentucky, determined. With everything to his name stuffed in the mute compartment of his trombone case, he stands in front of the bus depot wondering where to go. No friends in town; he's burned all of them at least once. There is Aunt Clara in Queens but she also intends to have seen Flagg for the last time.

This is his last chance. Now's the time, there will be no other. Having been forever on the road, Flagg knows New York no better than any other city—only certain hotels and corners which should be avoided if he is to succeed. He would like to listen to some sides, maybe smoke a little grass; preferably with a broad. Being nothing in this town, without money, friends, home, or a job is very scary. Flagg is scared . . . to death. He wants a fix.

To cool himself out, he decides on a stroll around Times Square. A plump old couple under five feet look at a window with mountains of cheap electronic gadgets on sale because "EVERYTHING ABSOLUTELY MUST GO." They are speaking Romanian or some language like that. They hold hands for a while. He stares at them, and at the sign.

Then, into an "art book" store, lining up with dead-cigar-mouth men browsing through things like *Pirate* and *Peek-a-boo.* When he finds himself even interested in a magazine called *Male,* he moves on. Flagg is very horny off dope and out of jail.

He spends ten dimes in an amusement gallery, trying to make fifteen runs on a baseball machine. Twelve is the best he can do. On the way out, Flagg notices somebody else's snot on his batting hand. He orders two double Old Bush-mills at the first available bar.

He has lunch alone in an Automat. Then into a White Rose for a few forty-cent shots. Making two more bar stops on the way, he settles near the Hudson River Day Line pier. After watching the garbage float for a while, he closes his eyes until a cop prods him. Move on! A double feature on 42nd Street is the rest of the afternoon.

Ten bucks gets him a weekend room in a flophouse on the West Side. He'll stay out of the ghetto—there's too much dope around.

Having been briefed on procedure by a faggot in Lexington, Flagg goes down to Welfare the next morning. He waits his turn. The others are either old or speak Spanish. There are many of them and they all look square and unhappy. So many children . . . what do they do if they get turned down?

He had to get out of there. There must be another way. I don't know how, but not welfare with these people. Maybe a coffee-shop gig in the East Village, work in a music store—anything. He splits. It's union day anyway. There will be familiar faces on the exchange floor.

Hey, there's Joey. Joey, baby . . . haven't seen you in years. Howya doin' man, you lookin' good.

Well if it isn't Flagg? First time they've met since Flagg stole Joey's horn from Birdland last year. Flagg mailed him the pawn ticket and figured that squared things. He hasn't thought about it since. Joey has. Well—uh, good to see you too Flagg, uh, there's my man over there with a gig for me. Later!

The afternoon goes much the same way. The few cats who do welcome him are scratching themselves and look sleepy. The sharp stud carrying a pair of drumsticks, wearing a shiny suit, white on white tie and shades is also glad to see Flagg. This man flashes him a very big smile.

Flagg goes upstairs to look for a phone, careful to avoid union officials who know him well for his unpaid dues and fines. He calls Aunt Clara . . . maybe she'll understand, put him up for a few weeks so's he can get himself together.

He dials her number a couple of times, then remembers she works. He calls there and says hello, he's back. She's busy and can't talk now. He'd like to see her. She's working late tonight and will be in the country over the weekend, Easter weekend. Call her on Monday. By the way . . . your mother sent you a little money from Chicago and why don't you straighten out and stop killing her bit by bit. No, he couldn't have the money before Monday. Can't you think of someone else besides yourself—ever? Call me Monday!

There is a small cockroach on the counter where he eats a greasy dinner. He buys some magazines and goes to the room, hoping to read, but the smell of armpit and mildew gets to him. Why not practice? With a cup mute stuffed as tight as possible in the bell, he plays a few scales until a knock on the door. Cut it out, the man says.

He goes out for a walk and it isn't long before he finds someone who knows his name and is glad to see him. Well, just this once. . . .

New York is a ghost town the next morning. Everybody is somewhere else for the weekend. West Side streets are deserted and the sun shines brightly on them with the first hint of summer. Flagg wakes up late, in a sweat from the radiator, hissing steam despite the weather.

Almost broke. Six dollars, some change and a half-empty pack of Camels, that's all until Monday. Maybe he should just buy a bag of dope with it and stop fooling around. No. He had promised himself only that one. He is shaky but not sick; he doesn't need a shot. Everybody has to pay dues sometimes and he certainly owes one lousy weekend. Besides, this is New York. There are lots of things to do.

He walks to the UN and sits in the park for an hour, then to Macy's where everybody is doing last-minute Easter shopping. It is very crowded and they all seem happy having friends and places to go. The only people he knows are dope fiends.

Sitting on a park bench near the zoo, watching the kids with balloons and little dogs. Girls in mini-skirts . . . Jeezus, he needs a woman. Flagg buys a hotdog with sauerkraut and a Coke from a Puerto Rican with an umbrella over his little cart. The Puerto Rican looks strung out.

Sweating, he walks up Fifth Avenue towards the Metropolitan Museum. Inside it's boring except for a girl with long legs and a short skirt sketching in front of a Rembrandt. She is very engrossed, probably no more than twenty. Despite the No Smoking sign, she has a lit cigarette in her mouth which, from the sweet odor, is obviously part pot. These kids today are something else. Should he strike up a conversation? What could he say? "Hi, my name is Flagg and I'm just out of jail." No good!

Her purse is unguarded so he swings with it. Now why did he do that? He's only stolen for one reason in his life and that's supposed to be over with. He drops it near the door, everything still in it but a twenty-dollar bill which buys him a Julie Christie movie, a big German dinner, a pint of house vodka and a taxi ride to his room. He is proud of himself. He didn't cop. He could have but he didn't. A broken pattern; hope.

By ten he has emptied the jug and fallen asleep. He dreams of being tickled by the girl in the museum. She is nude and giggling like mad. As he begins making love to her, she snarls, "You bastard: you stole my bloody twenty quid." She turns into Julie Christie and bites him. He comes. There are teeth marks on his thigh and something gray and quick scurries to a corner. His hands shake so badly he can hardly tie his shoelaces.

Sunday is cooler. The park is packed with hippies near the Tavern on the Green; a Be-in, he is told. People are giving chocolate bars, flowers, and other little presents to passing strangers. A girl with stringy hair, wearing only an Indian shirt, plants a flower in a policeman's badge. He smiles at her.

There must be a hundred flower children dancing in a circle. After a signal they converge towards each other, into a hugging and laughing ball. Ordinary people are playing catch and leap-frog with their kids. Dogs run around. Guys with beards fly peace kites.

Two kids play guitars together, singing along. One of them keeps referring to his axe as a "tuigar." Flagg feels like blowing. He wishes he had his horn—but he'd probably be too up-tight anyway.

The smell of grass is everywhere in the spring air. When someone offers him a poke, he takes it. Why not? It's so ridiculously harmless. Why couldn't he have just stopped with that? Do any of these kids take off? . . . What a bore to always think of only that one thing. Man, he must be sick. What was it he'd read somewhere? Some doctor said that the drug addict has the "horror of euphoric memory." Just stop and think about dope for a second; it's perfect. It's always there, any time any little thing goes wrong . . .

bingo . . . the bells start ringing and you know that all of the anxiety, the pain—whatever—can disappear. That knowledge is a fucking drag.

A few hours later, Flagg loses Sunday too, without a fight. Three in a row.

Later, just wandering—"hanging-out," he calls it—he decides to try Aunt Clara again. He finds a phone booth in the lobby of the Great Northern Hotel. Her line is busy. He hears music from Fine Sound Studio "A" next door. A red light flashes the warning "RECORDING." The line is still busy. The light goes off.

. . . Through the door hesitatingly . . . it is Duke Ellington with his full band and a chorus recording some kind of religious piece. The energy, precision, and warmth of the music gives Flagg goose bumps. He forgets about being lonely, scared, angry, and the rest of it.

The chorus rises. After a few directions from Duke and a slate from the control booth, they begin to chant: slowly, *a capella:* "FREE-DOM . . . FREE-DOM." Flagg stands in a corner listening and nodding for God knows how long.

From *New Life* (ARC newsletter):

America was founded on this statement: *In God We Trust* . . . in our American schools our children don't learn of/can't talk about/or pray to that God. Our children can sit in front of a "mini-skirted" teacher and peer under her dress, learn about swearing, about the finer points of sex, and anything else but about that God—in whom "we trust."

This is an age of wars and conflicts and strifes; of discrimination and rioting and looting; of Christiandom vs. Islam; communism vs. democracy; black vs. white; poverty vs. wealth; of shifting blame and responsibility from one to the other and of choosing sides.

The other day I was asked what side I am on, and this is my answer:

I will not fight any particular ethnic, religious, or political group, although I have not been treated fairly by any. To be sure, I do feel the pangs of prejudiceness and discrimination because I am a Negro living in a predominately white society. I do also feel the pressures and problems that have been created by the distinction between race, religion and creed. All of us cannot be/nor do some of us want to be Martin Luther Kings, Rap Browns, Malcom Xs, Lyndon Johnsons, five per centers, black militants, or Ku Kluxers because somebody has to "stay home and watch the store."

What am I fighting against? I am fighting against the conditions that result from all of the chaos and confusion. I am fighting on God's side in opposition to anything that my bible tells me is wrong . . . whether it be black, white, blue, green, or purple. However due to my limitation of power, influence, and strength, I am waging my war on four fronts . . . in my immediate neighborhood.

I am fighting against the top—In helping to provide addict rehabilitation, I fight every step of the way to acquire operational funds; I fight against ignorant powers that would impose methadon-maintenance as *the solution* to heroin-addiction; against public leaders who are all too often ignorant of the misery and frustration that cause addicts to revert to drug-dependence behavior. I even fight the NYC Police Department, out of my own ignorance of the "finer" details involved in making narcotic arrests and getting convictions. And I fight my own community because it has been led to believe: "once an addict, always an addict."

I am fighting against the bottom—the crummy building I live in . . . reeking with the smell of urine, the dirty floors and broken windows, the backyard that's littered with garbage; the huge rats living inside its walls that sleep all day and work all night—foraging food in the form of human flesh; the millions of cock-roaches crawling over me when I'm asleep, sharing my coffee when I'm awake, tumbling into my guests drink when I entertain; and the huge flies and tiny mosquitoes that come through my window—left open in summer heat so that I can breathe "fresh pollution"—

I am fighting against the inside—offtimes, my

supervisors, my staff, and even the people that I am trying to help don't understand my philosophy. I must then take valuable time away from my fighting progress and explain, re-interpret—this article results from that; and there are those who, even after being helped, remain ungrateful—voicing condemnation for the program and everything connected with it . . . especially me—and I fight against something that swells inside me . . .

I am fighting against the outside—the active drug-users that beat a steady path to my rooftop . . . two . . . three . . . four . . . five times or more a day to perform their rituals with the heroin-god; I fight the constant fear that, surely, soon a lighted cigarette will slip from near-paralyzed fingers and bring all our lives to a sudden, dramatic, fiery exclamation point . . . or again, perhaps, even my own 15 year-old might be "drawn" into the half-way world of the living dead.

The whole street scene—the drunk, pissing against a church wall, or in the door-way, or in my hallway; the 15 year-old boy carrying a woman's purse . . . fading in the distance . . . pursued by a woman . . . yelling, "stop thief" . . . the promiscuious lovers . . . in the airshaft; the quarreling lovers . . . leaning on the car; the "young men" making "love" across the street; the teen-age junkie-couples, who have established "residence" in a vacant house and are playing "man and wife" . . . ; the dope pusher who "sets up shop" under my window and "deals like he has a license"; the winos who use my stoop for a whiskey bar, and break the empty bottles on the curb . . . and the mysterious Cadillac that pulls up to the pusher—

puncturing a tire on the broken glass. The huge dice-game up the street that the police can't seem to ever break up; the little kids, who should have been in bed hours ago—playing in between cars that are driven much too fast in a side street shattering the night with the sound of screeching tires —digging the whole scene.

The gloomy, defeated, hopeless looks on neighborhood faces that will change only with the sounds of gunfire, screams, or crushing metal . . . that will surely come before the night is over. I am fighting against the foul smell of saturday-night garbage and a thousand empty whiskey bottles and beer-cans—that tell me that somebody spent more than they could afford—these empties will spoil an otherwise, cheery Sunday morning; a trail of blood that leads towards the hospital, and the puddle indicating that "he didn't make it."

I am fighting against conditions that allow a dead junkie to lay on a roof-top for nearly twelve hours—until the morgue wagon "gets around to picking him up" . . . and the condition that causes him to be there in the first place; against the suspense of waiting for an ambulance to arrive and "plug up a hole" while the victim's life gushes forth red and spills into a dirty gutter—washing on into the Hudson River on the next flush of a slum toilet.

These conditions have many forms . . . I am fighting against the whole system . . . the things I see, feel, smell, hear, and taste. I am fighting against these things because I have been told that man is the highest form of God's creation and that He thought so much of man that He sent his own (only) son into the world to see, feel, smell, hear, and taste these same things . . . and to die so that I might not be humiliated, overcome, and destroyed . . . . and so that I might win this fight. If God did this for me, then I must fight to see if my life, which he considered valuable enough to die for, can have any positive value upon someone else's . . .

JAMES ALLEN

2
The Next Flush

IKE

"Unfortunately, I was very lucky at breakin' the law. In all my life I've only been arrested twenty-two times." The new Ike Houston is neatly togged in a shiny gray suit, behind the reception desk. His thick head of oily curls and his Van Dyke are carefully trimmed. He speaks with a sparkle in his eyes, which are clear and look right at me.

"Look; a drug addict who will finally leave drugs alone is a pretty slick dude. If he's survived ten, fifteen, or twenty years of shootin dope, he's got to be strong, he's got to be smart, and he's got to be lucky. Now, if he would just remember all the things he did when he used drugs and just turn 'em over . . ." He turns a hand slowly, palm up, with a sly smile.

". . . In other words, do the same things but don't break the law when you do them. I feel he will be very successful because he has such a . . . look, I'll give it to you like this. When I was gettin' arrested all the time, I figured I'd better learn somethin' about the law since I was breakin' it constantly. And I got to know about as much about it as . . . why, if I get arrested and go down to the courthouse, the lawyers see me and they say right away, 'Oh. Okay. Here's this guy again. Let him take his own case.'

"I figured I better learn what's goin' on because if somethin' goes wrong *I'm* the one that's gonna do all the time. I knew I had to hit the judge with somethin' he ain't used to.

I can't hit him with that same old story, 'Your Honor, please give me a break.' No, no. Can't give him that. That's foolish. So I . . . excuse me."

The phone. Ike mans the switchboard at the Addicts Rehabilitation Center. "May I help you? . . . No, I'm sorry. We can't do anything like that for your son. What we can do is help him get into a hospital . . . Yes, that's right, but he'll have to come in person . . . There is a wait, that's right ma'am, but we can usually cut it a little short . . . probably by Monday. May I have your name please?"

As Ike takes care of business, people pass through the spare, newly painted reception room. Going out the door, they sign their names, time of day, and the reason for leaving. There is much giving of skin. The vernacular is heavy. The Formica top of Ike's desk sags noticeably over an underdesigned span. The radiator hisses, too hot. Across 123rd Street, a black lady is pressing clothes under a bare light bulb in "Bea's Laundry." The pedestrians are unusually white for Harlem; cops from the 28th Precinct down the block.

The aquarium filter next to Ike all but drowns out the Wilson Pickett records floating in from the day room where the usual cauldron of coffee is hot and ready. The amount of coffee and cigarettes consumed per capita at ARC must be among the best in the nation. How benign these evils seem up here. Pneumonia is nothing compared to terminal cancer.

The day room walls are covered with posters, drawings, and signs. Five programmers are settled in comfortable, beat-up furniture, two playing chess. An enormous lady with teeth missing, partly burned white, is reading the *Daily News* way out in front of her big stomach. She smiles at me. A short, extremely black guy, wearing an embroidered Black Muslim cap, doesn't.

The bulletin board is covered by neatly typed lists of names and duties for the week, and the following:

ABOUT ARC

WHO:	Fourteen former addicts, three part time professional consultants and one full time, working under the supervision of the Manhattan Christian Reformed Church.
WHAT:	A program of rehabilitation to help addicts unlearn negative habits acquired during the period of addiction, and further assist these in developing new patterns of thought and action so that they can assume more respectful positions within the home environment.
WHEN:	During the weeks immediately following discharge from hospital (or prison) after these addicts return home. Daycare: 85 hours seven days weekly.
RESIDENCE:	Available to carefully selected persons. Open Meetings: Monday and Wednesday evenings, 8 P.M. at 201 West 122 St. Room 2-A. Open to all persons interested in the addiction problem.
WHERE:	Daycare: 253 W. 123 St. Residence: 255 W. 123 St.
HOW:	Referrals to hospital services for addicted persons; speakers, panelists, advisors, consultants, and training for interested groups and group workers.

Like most of the guys at ARC, Ike had absolutely no idea what he was getting into. Junk was just around all the time, that's all, and in 1947 at the age of twenty-four—old for Harlem—it found him. He'd been smoking reefer routinely for years when, at a party, he spotted a couple of guys sneaking off to the bathroom. Thinking of a smoke, he followed. They were snorting. He went along with the program. The stuff made him sick and very thirsty. Three times he drank a Coke and brought it right back up. Then he was thirsty again. And sick.

A few days later, on the street taking numbers as usual, Ike bumped into one of the guys from the john. "Man," he said, "I don' want any more of that stuff. That crap got me sick."

"No, baby," the guy answered. "You ought to try it again. It really gets you high. You only got sick because you never did it before."

Ike tried again and it was better. Numbers were pretty free and easy back then (still only a misdemeanor), and a young, intelligent, enterprising and energetic hustler like Ike could make heavy bread. Supporting his new-found fun was no problem. But he didn't know about the escalation. Ike thought it was like reefer. He'd get high, he'd come down, he'd get high again, and it was all right.

He particularly looked forward to his six o'clock taste, after the last number was out. One afternoon, though, his wife stopped him on the street, on her way home with groceries. She wanted to go to the movies and, instead of snorting, he went straight downtown with her. The November chill seemed extreme to Ike on line in front of the Roxy. Inside, watching *Unconquered* with Susan Hayward and Gary Cooper, it was even cooler. He thought it was a cold coming on.

Ike was used to neighborhood guys hitting on him for a dollar all the time. That's what a cap (one high) cost in the forties. "Man, lay a bean on me. I'm sick," they'd rasp out. Ike always figured they knew he was a soft touch with a pocket full of bills, he knew they weren't really sick but always gave them at least fifty cents anyway. He thought he had a cold, walking out on *Unconquered*. His wife hailed a cab.

Ike was born, raised, and hustled on the same block. Everybody knew him and the street was popping with friends as the taxi pulled in front of his door. Ike doubled up in the back seat. His wife called some of the guys over from the stoop next door. As they helped him upstairs, one dude nudged him, "What's the matter, man? Ain't you got no money?"

"Money? What, you kiddin' me?" Ike answered. "What you talkin' about, money? I got money. What's money got to do with it?"

"Then why don' you go an' take care of business?"

"Man, what you talkin' about?"

"Jim, you sick."

"I know I'm sick, Jack. You ain't tellin' me nothin'."

"Then why don' you go an' get some stuff?"

"What you mean, get me some stuff?"

"When did you have some stuff last?"

"When did I have some heroin, you mean? It must have been around 11:30 or 12:00."

"Why didn't you get no more?"

"I—I don' know . . . I went to the movies."

"Man, are you kiddin'? You got a habit. Give me some scratch and I'll get you a cap."

His wife came from the kitchen with a pot of tea. Ike had snorted and was no longer cold. "What happened?" she asked. "You look fine now."

"Yeah," Ike was trying to think. "I *feel* fine."

PANCHO

In Mexico we have dope all year round. I'm talkin' about heroin. They got the best heroin there. Here they have junk from overseas and it's cut, but in Mexico, where I come from, it's pure dope.

I was born in Mexico and raised in El Paso, two blocks from Mexico. So that means we can cross over a lot—any time. The poverty there—if you've ever been to Juarez you know what I'm talkin' about—it's just dirt and a lot of people who don't have enough money to live with. And that's what I try to tell the guys here at ARC—they ain't as bad off as they think.

The first time I fixed I was twenty-one. But I had been smoking pot, sniffing gas, taking pills, drinking. . . . I didn't get into the heavy stuff until later, when I went to California. You see when I was fifteen I was the leader of a gang. I used to have some broads working the doctors in El Paso, Texas. I wasn't usin' nothin' then. These girls would go to a doctor, make it with him in his office and come back with the scrips. Then we'd go to the drugstore and we'd be legit. The girl would buy the stuff and it would cost me four, five bucks. She would give me the stuff and I would sell it. I was makin' good money like that. All I had to do was keep producin' different girls for the doctors.

The broads did it for the gang, you know, and me—I was the gang leader. They was happy enough to perform. They had some excitement and all. We'd party all the time. We always had a lot of pot. I was dealin' in pot at the time too. Everythin' was exciting.

We had fights all over. We was members of the Seven-Eleven gang back in El Paso; we controlled Washington Park.

There was me and my brother and five sisters in the family. I'm what you call a black sheep. And I'm happy I'm the one, you know, because I can't see one of my brothers or sisters goin' through what I did.

I'm thirty-six now and I've been tryin' to get away from dope since 1960. I tried this Narcotics Anonymous. I liked what they said; you know, "God, lend me the serenity to accept the things I cannot change, courage to change the things I can." I tried. I was the outside sponsor of a penitentiary. I was clean, you understand, but I didn't know anybody. When I walked out of the pen I was by myself. But I got a lot of friends of mine still inside, people with the same problem as me, people who know what I'm talkin' about. So I become the outside sponsor, I go back once a week and show them I'm still clean—we help each other. And I have to associate myself with what's next to us—I really wanted to stay clean, you understand? The Alcoholics Anonymous. Although they tried to understand my problem, they really couldn't. They gave me a corner, you know, like a boxer in a ring. They accepted me for what I was. They said, "You have a disease just like we do, but you are from a different walk of life so we really can't understand you but we can give you the understanding we give our own kind and from here you can operate in the penitentiary."

Mr. C. J. McCleary was mayor of the town—Anthony, Texas—still is I think. He'd been an FBI agent for twenty-five years. He set up this NA program. He said he got so tired putting so many addicts in the pen that he volunteered for penitentiary work. The pen we are talkin' about is twelve miles outside of El Paso in La Tuna, Texas. Mr. McCleary was interested in me. He used to come to my house from Anthony to pick me up so I could go to meetings. He wants to help. He sees there is no help for the addict. There's help here in New York, but practically nowhere else. That's why I came to New York. It's like Hollywood. What do you hear about Hollywood? Movie stars. You hear about drugs, and help for them—that's New York.

But I'm jumpin' around a lot . . . I left El Paso with my gang—we all went together. When we got to L. A. I found I could make easy money doin' the same things I was doin' in El Paso. We hung around Bunker Hill—a lot of action. Guys from all over—North Hollywood, Watts—all over, come to score there. I was right in the middle of it with my gang. All my gang came to L. A. and a lot of them are still in prison in California—San Quentin, Folsom.

Right away, I ran into some broads workin' on a Broadway show—you know, strip teasers. They would come and tell me, "Hey, honey child, I want to score for some shit." I see those big bodies as mine. I say, wow—swingin' . . . you know. Everythin' is GOIN'! And then they take me to those swanky places out there—man, they treated me like I was a king.

I'd started fixin' myself by then. I really liked what was goin' on. At the time, I really liked it. I believe that anybody who starts usin' drugs likes the game—what's in it. And you can't help anyone until that drops off. You gotta start gettin' tired—and then you gotta start gettin' tired of bein' tired of bein' tired. You get sick and tired of bein' tired and sick. That's when we can help. A lot of guys back then used to tell me that they wished they could be like me—for one reason or another they weren't fixin'. A lot of them ended up in the pen anyway—for somethin' else. Now I know different, but I really felt big then.

I was a big man in L. A. for a while. The way I got in that position . . . just before I came out of the joint they had busted three big guys; I'm talkin' about *big* connections. Big-time connections, man. So when I get out on the street, some people I know, they say . . . well, there it is, man. Run!

Well, I've been an organizer all my life. I've been a gang leader and that means I can control guys. I shot in there. I covered Hollywood, North Hollywood, Sunset Strip, a little bit through Watts. It wasn't long before I had forty guys on the street sellin' dope. The reason it was so easy for me was that I happened to come in when the big people were gone.

These big people had been there for five, seven, ten years. I started medium, not big, but soon the business people saw that I could handle it. They said, yeah man, go ahead!

These people are respectable people; businessmen. They shake your hand. Actually, they were people from Mexico; strong people, responsible, established in L. A. They don't have to touch anything. They've got farms over in Mexico where they raise it, you understand, so they can get anybody in the streets, clean him up, and say I want you to take this package with you—it's so easy.

We're talkin' about big-time people, not people like me. They've been at this years and years. They got their stuff from Mexico, from Castro Cuba, and they use guys like me to get it on the street.

I've been talkin' about some of the better times, but by the same token I've been on skid rows, I've been ridin' freight trains. Fear, fear has driven me.

I was doin' good. I got money, piles of bread all over, clothes, two or three cars, broads. Then the mouthpiece calls and says, "Go! Split!" I don't ask no more. I know what he means by that. The broad goes in one car, I go in another—it's my third wife I'm talkin' about. Two cars to flank, you know, because I don't want to carry a bunch of stuff bein' they after me as it is.

The broad's got everythin', you know what I mean? She's drivin' in front. I got some clothes with me—that's all. I'm followin'. At that time I was real straight. We got two fine cars—a Ford and a Mercury. This is about 1958-59. We wound up in Phoenix, just coastin' around. We got rid of the cars, but we still got a bunch of dope and a bunch of money.

We checked into a motel with a swimmin' pool and everythin'. I was just layin' there; shootin' stuff, shootin' stuff, shootin' stuff. She was sayin' all the time, "Come on man, let's go here, let's go there, let's do this, let's do that." She wasn't usin' stuff then and I was sayin', "Oh come on honey, here's some money—go." I didn't want to go to the movies or anythin'. I just laid-in all day and all night, shootin' up.

The lawyer is makin' phone calls—not from his own phone. My wife would always answer. It was definite that I had to stay out of L. A. Definite! But I still had a bunch of dope and I know I'm not goin' to shoot it all, and I really shouldn't be carryin' it around . . . so I start lookin' around Phoenix.

Well, I went to buy some clothes one day and I met this friend of mine. It didn't take me no time to get this guy dealin' stuff for me. I tol' him I don' want him dealin' himself. He should get guys pushin' on the street for him. I said, "I'll give it to you for five dollars, you give it to the other guys for seven-fifty and the guy who sells it will get ten or maybe twelve on the street. Plus, you can give it a little more of a cut in between."

So, before I knew it, I'm makin' money in Phoenix, Arizona. I was doin' okay, but the time came—and it *will* come—when the dope was out . . . no more dope. Wow, what a drag. I turned to terpo-hydrate and codeine—and I find myself drinkin' alcohol behind it.

My wife sees me become a different person, right in front of her eyes, from an addict to an alcoholic—drugstore plus alcohol, you understand? I changed overnight. She couldn't cope with me on alcohol. We stayed around Phoenix and money-wise we was still okay. But I'm steadily throwin' money away and after a while she gives me an allotment—a hundred a day. That's all I could spend—a hundred a day. And I could kill a hundred a day like nothin' and come back for more. Actually, what I was doin' was bein' a big shot, you know, throwin' money away, still livin' in that dream world of bein' on Sunset Strip, Jerry Lewis and all those actors right next to me. But it's not there any more. And fear is drivin', fear is drivin', fear is drivin'. I became an alcoholic too.

IKE

The old Ike said, "Man, I'm gettin' tired of this stuff. It's costin' me four, five dollars a day."

His friend answered, "Why don' you shoot it? You only need half a cap that way."

The idea of saving bread made sense. They went to visit some dude who had a set of works. Ike stayed tore-up half the night. "Oh my goodness," he reasoned to himself, "and I saved three dollars."

But it will build. Before long, Ike was taking off four times a day. It happened so gradually he hardly noticed. Soon it hit ten dollars a day. But there was plenty of money in his pocket, he felt fine, could afford sharp clothes and he had a lot of friends. He was a happy, successful young man. He felt sorry for all the squares who didn't know any better than going to work downtown on the subway each day. What a dumb life! Sweeping floors, delivering groceries, sitting in men's rooms, pushing a cart in the garment district. He was smarter than that; slick; with the in-crowd.

Ike's son had long hair and he liked it that way. His wife and mother-in-law differed and there were constant arguments about the desirability of a trim. On his son's second birthday, Ike saw his wife walking down the street holding some little boy in her arms. He thought it was a neighborhood kid and didn't pay him any mind as he spoke to her. But it was his with short hair. Ike didn't yell or argue. He rarely argued with his old lady any more. On, aggravations vanish. He could watch a movie or just sit and scratch.

One night, Ike was baby-sitting with that urge. There was nothing in the house and, since his son was asleep anyway, he split to score. (It wouldn't take all that long.) But the boy woke up in a sweat, began to cry and, by the time Ike's old lady got home, was running a good temperature. When he returned about four he found the note and made it right over to the hospital.

After his son recovered from the pneumonia Ike decided he'd better kick. By now he had proper respect for the shit shooting in his veins. He stopped the same way he started. Just stopped. Cold turkey. It wasn't really as bad as all that. A stomachache, not much food or sleep for a week and a general nervousness for some days after that. When he came out on the street again, Ike was clean.

He decided to move. Everybody knew him on that block and they hit on him for money all the time, especially if he'd had a good day with the numbers. But the bad days he'd have to carry all by himself. So he said, "Phooey with this," and moved on down to 98th Street, his mother's neighborhood. Although he saw drug addicts every day, he never took off himself. It never occurred to him from 1950 to 1957, not one bag of dope as he developed another good numbers business, including the operation of two candy-store fronts.

He would have to turn the numbers money over to the banker, less commission, every morning. But while he had it he'd put it to work. Say the day's take was three hundred dollars. It was his until the morning and he could pass a note for some of it. On Friday, he could juggle for the whole weekend. He'd buy twenty cases of wine and stash them in a basement. The winos are too busy drinking instead of thinking, "Oh, it's getting late and it's Saturday night, I'll buy three bottles for tomorrow." By the time they look up it's Sunday. Ike never had any left on Monday morning. The old Ike was a good hustler.

He was arrested a lot. Being caught with numbers in those days, outside of the nuisance, wasn't a particularly big thing. He'd go to jail, bail would be posted for him, and he'd come right back out again. He didn't really know what jail was, other than being booked. And this was mostly in the beginning when he was new in the neighborhood, before he got his "okay" from the police department. The okay cost him five hundred dollars on the first and fifteenth of every month. As long as he paid, no cop would bother him in his hallway or candy stores. He was okay with the precinct, the division, and downtown. Out of eight officers at headquarters, two were on his payroll and they'd always pull Ike's coat before some action was planned for uptown. The customers kept coming since they knew the cop on the corner wasn't going to run in right behind them. Business conditions were bullish on West 98th Street.

But, in 1956, urban renewal started tearing the neighborhood down in favor of Park West Village. Just about all the hustling people moved up between 110th and 116th Street. Competition up there was ridiculous. Ike laid back. His six-hundred-dollar bankroll went fast and before long he was searching around for new opportunities. Just about broke, he ran into an old friend. "Man, what you doin'?" he asked Ike.

"I ain't doin' nothin'."

"Hey, Jim, why don' you get yourself some dope and push it?"

"You gotta be kiddin', man. I don't know nothin' about pushin' dope." Getting a "job" never occurred to Ike.

The cat reminded him, "Didn't you come from uptown, originally? Man, that's where *all* the deals is. You can go up there and get a connection. Everybody knows you up there."

Thinking about the money he was spending every day playing the numbers and jiving in crap games, he went uptown. Sure enough, some of the biggest dealers were guys he grew up with. They were glad to sell him.

He sold dope for the rest of 1956 without using any. He was too kind. If a guy would cry sick with only three dollars, Ike would say, "Oh well, here. Take a bag anyway." The news traveled. "If you're sick, man, see Ike. He's the type of dude who'll feel sorry for you." Because of his reputation, the stick-up boys never bothered him, and besides he was making good bread anyway.

One day a dude came up to him and said, "Man, I ain't got but two dollars. Jim, why don't you take my two dollars and when you get off, give me a little taste from your bag?"

"When *I* get off? From my bag? Man, you know I don't. . . ." Then Ike thought, "Oh shit, I'm sick and tired of *givin'* my dope away. Why give this guy a five-dollar bag for two? Yeah—I think I will take a taste." And Ike was on another jones.

By 1960 he was no longer so sharp. His habit was costing forty to fifty dollars a day. He had drifted apart from his wife, ending that problem but also leaving him homeless. He couldn't find a hustle. He slept around; with friends, relatives, or on roofs. It had happened so slowly, inevitably, that his past affluence seemed a dream, only half-remembered. He had become a leper, a walking zombie. A dope fiend.

Ike pressed on. Down 57th Street, six new suits over his arm, in the middle of the night. A panic was on. The skin on his light brown, freckled face was tightly drawn, his cheeks hollow. He was dressed in beat suntans and a torn basketball jacket, too light for the weather and inappropriate to the neighborhood. Of course a cop stopped him.

"What was I thinkin' of, anyway?" Ike said to himself in the precinct bullpen. "How'm I goin' to get out of *this* one?" He looked his situation over. "Oh. I know what I'll do," he said aloud, pointing a forefinger up with the inspiration.

As the cop wrote up the charges, Ike started crying, rubbing his hands nervously, and speaking in a Spanish accent. "Please officer. Please don' fingerpreent me . . . please officer . . . because I gonna be in a lotta trouble if they sen' me bock to Cooba. Please don' lock me up . . . please don' because I came in off a sheep an' I jump the sheep, an' . . . ." Castro had just taken Cuba.

The cop was very happy. My goodness, this was going to be an easy one. Why would this guy confess to being an alien unless he was? In addition to suspicion of robbery, he added the charge of unregistered alien.

Ike resumed his Cuban grovel, appearing terribly nervous. "I tell you what . . . I tell you . . . I sign eet an' then you let me go maybe, because I no get een trouble no more . . . I promees." He signs the confession, nodding, friendly to the officer.

The FBI as well as the Immigration people were in court the next day to check this alien out. But so was Ike's lawyer with his birth certificate: born in Harlem, USA. The arresting officer used all of his self-control as he said, "Boy, I oughta break your neck." Ike looked at him with a good American sneer: "What? Are you kiddin' me?"

In a confession, if one part is a lie, how about the rest of it? The lawyer, the judge, and the assistant D. A. held a short conference and decided the case had to be thrown out. This man is a bona fide citizen. Everybody looks unhappy as Ike says, "Your Honor, I'd confess to anything once they get to kickin' and beatin' on me. They beat me half to death in the precinct."

Six months later, he wasn't at all unhappy when he was busted with a bag of heroin and sent to the Federal hospital in Lexington, Kentucky. He stayed four months and fifteen days and came out physically clean.

He tried to get back into numbers but no controller would put him in a hallway. Since he knew all the cheats and crooks from being in it since a kid, nobody trusted him. So he stole some more from parked cars, shoplifted, sneak-thiefed banks. A very successful thief, he supported his brand new habit: cocaine.

Strictly speaking, coke is not habit-forming. When you stop you don't vomit or anything and you can eat, too. But it's difficult or impossible to control your limbs and the letdown is something awful.

Another trouble with cocaine—"the sport of the gods"—is that it is terribly expensive. You shoot a ten-dollar cap of coke at three o'clock. Four and a half minutes later, that's all you're going to get for your ten bucks. It's one hell of a four and a half minutes, though, and if a real coke head has two hundred dollars in his pocket he's quite likely to keep on shooting every four and a half minutes until it runs out.

Ike shot coke for a whole year, stealing every day. He'd sneak into office buildings, find things in unlocked desk drawers or forgotten purses. But he'd think—after he was high—maybe the woman was Negro and had five kids or something.

One particular purse had only twenty-two dollars in it. He saw by the identification that the owner lived on 120th Street and St. Nicholas Avenue. A few hours after stealing it, he managed to take off a color television set, fencing it for $175, so he decided to take the girl back her twenty-two dollars. He rang her bell; "You lost your pocketbook, didn't you?" He handed her the bag. She stared at him.

Ike became embarrassed. "I, er . . . you know, . . . I'm a drug addict and I . . . er, had to have some money. . . . I, uh . . . er, hope I didn't inconvenience you."

She said, "You look like such a nice fellow. Why do you use drugs?" Ike couldn't wait to split.

As soon as possible he got high; he felt so guilty. And it occurred to him that if he could stop stealing, maybe he wouldn't use drugs any more.

Two weeks of shooting dope and stealing later, he got busted again. Out of jail this time, he wasn't going to steal anything—nothing. He might have it made if he could just keep from stealing. All his friends were making bets—they knew he was going to take somebody's money—because he only had one pair of shoes, one pair of pants, an old raincoat—and Ike was too proud to beg. He went over to Welfare. The man at the office said go see Mr. James Allen at the Addicts Rehabilitation Center. . . .

PANCHO

I wound up in a Texas hospital, being treated for alcoholism plus drug addiction and a third degree burn. I went through a lot of misery and pain, but when I got out of the hospital, I started drinkin' and fixin' again. It was a duet.

You see, you can't quit drugs alone. Man, you'll never make it, unless you get saved by God. But on your own you'll never make it—and that's what I was tryin' to do.

Then I bumped into an old friend of mine. He's what you call a player—a guy from Abilene, Texas. My friend Harry. He plays the broads. He was a big man, an intelligent man, a good-looking man. He knows how to size up broads, just as I know how to size up dope fiends. He gets money from broads.

Harry liked my style. We became like brothers. Imagine, a big man like that. That's when I started sellin' signs and ridin' airplanes.

I sold signs that turned in the wind for American Advertising. My friend Harry was the manager for the Western region. It's a big business, they got their own airplanes and everything, and here I was a no-good guy, a dope fiend with a seventh-grade education. So I said, "Thank you God, thank you. I know somebody up there likes me—thank you."

Everybody in the company knew what I used to be, but they gave me a chance. They said, "Look at him now." I bought a hundred-dollar suit, shoes—everything—with my money, my bread; I *earned* this bread.

It was big business, man. I was taking a little terp sometimes—I wasn't honest with myself—but I was finding out that I could function in this square world and I found I could do the job and be with these big business people and they would listen to what I had to say, regardless of my tattoos. I found out that I was okay—I could function out there. I could use all my dope-fiend keenness, all that hustlin' ability I had from the past, and just turn it around and use it legally.

I plug in my little projector and it's like a five-minute movie. I talk along with it. I say, "We've been in the neon business for the last thirty years and Mr. William F. Alexander, which is the president of our company—he came out with the impossible. He came out with a rotary sign and it turns with the wind. Now I'm goin' to say it again . . . it turns with the wind. You don't have to plug nothin' in—we got it fixed up—we put the sign out there and we bring all the customers you want. Let me show you what I mean."

I'm bein' a little shaky, you know, but I can do it. I plug the machine in and the picture comes on. . . . "Now this is Mr. William F. Alexander—he's been in the neon business for thirty years. . . . Now we have sign number one . . . see how beautiful it is . . . see the sign turnin' around. And you notice how it's turnin' with the wind . . . all it does is turn with the wind according to how the wind is, you know." And now you might say at this point, "How about earthquakes, tornadoes, hurricanes and things?" Well, one thing about this sign, it's insured. And it only can go so fast, 'cause if the wind is hard we got a bearin' that works against itself. Right now these signs are all over the place. We just opened on the West Coast and we already expanded ourselves from Abilene, Dallas, Fort Worth, into El Paso and we're in California too. We're working with the Roadway Inn people—they're expandin' . . . Incidentally—have you heard of Coca Cola? All over the world, right? Well do you know that every five seconds somewhere around the world there is something to be seen mentioning Coca Cola. That's advertising for you. But remember, we can bring customers to you, but it's up to you to bring 'em back. You still have to treat 'em nice. We can't do that for you. . . ."

Incidentally, I violated the law sellin' the signs too 'cause I sold one in Mexico—to Virginia Gomez. She's a very important woman, a very important woman in Mexico. I sold her a sign, smuggled it into Mexico. I bought off a man in the customs. This was a big man, in the clique of the president, you know? We bought him off—my friend Harry and me—tellin' him that we were givin' him a part of the action. Easy money, you know what I mean? I was tellin' him, well, "You and me. I'll get you the signs and I'll pass them across. You set it up over there."

But he was already goin' behind my back—see, what he wanted was just to get one of the signs over there so he could build his own. See, our patent was no good in Mexico. Anyway, this commander—the customs man—he takes me and my friend Harry around. Everybody salutes and—wow—I think I'm an ambassador or somethin'. And I made the biggest connection I could have when I met this man, this commander. He was a friend of the President of Mexico, man . . . the President of Mexico.

But one night Billie Sol Estes and his friends, they approach Harry at the Roadway Inn and offer him a deal. Harry don't want no part of it, though, and he says to me, "Let's go. Let's get out of here."

That's not Harry's stick. He operates by himself. When you work for a guy like Billie Sol, you know, you become a flunky. He's not that type. Harry's an adventurer you might say. If he needs somethin', baby he knows how to get it. He knows how to play girls. That's all his life, man. So he says, "Why get mixed up with all this stuff?" He left with some rich broad he met in a country club or someplace but I stayed. All the big people—Virginia Gomez, officials in the Mexican Government—they all liked me.

I was tellin' them, "Here's some money. I'm goin' to show you how to make some money." And these are intelligent people. I got connected with them from my sign, a sign they never heard about. Because it was even new in the United States at the time. It's all over the West Coast and they seen some possibilities in it. And here I'm goin' to these expensive places and they're givin' me playin' money and all.

But then that junk, man . . . somehow that dope got to me. I got shot down. A big bust, it was all over the paper, my picture and everythin'. Naturally this commander, he cuts me loose. He says, "Oh, no." I can't blame him. I went back to stuff, like I always do. I was still goin' to work, but I lost Pancho, you know. I'm ridin' around with my projector but I got a habit and it's not the same. The load is gettin' heavier and heavier.

Chacha was my connection. Everybody knows Chacha where I come from. She's a big-time connection. The FBI knows who I mean. They call her the "Queen of the Border." One day she says, when am I goin' to work for her? And I'm kinda ready to give in because the money is gettin' short.

So I finally agree. In El Paso, where I come from, you steal somethin' on the American side, take it to the Mexican side and she give you junk for it. When her warehouse gets full, you know, someone gotta take it out; washing machines, television sets, cameras. She has to sell 'em somewhere. Chacha sends me with her lieutenant; she's usin' me now and I know 'cause I wasn't born yesterday. But she's doin' it in the game way, you dig? She says, "Go with my boy here—help him." I'm a different type of guy, she tells me. "You're all right, you know. You're straight. I can trust you."

What she's tryin' to do is get me in her program, get me

involved. Somehow, somethin' happened and they caught us in Mexico with all that stolen property from the United States. I had my little five-hundred-dollar projector from American Advertising with me and they whammed that too. I came all over the papers again.

So I traveled some more with Harry—he'd played out this broad by then. I became an account executive in Phoenix, an executive on a magazine. I would go to a store and say, "We can put you in a magazine, on the front page cover, a picture of you—the works." All that sort of thing. "We'll fix you real nice." Which we did. I was registered with the Better Business Bureau, the chief of police and all this. Young people would come looking for a job and I would interview them. I had my own organization: bookkeeper, telephone girl, secretary.

Then I went out to California—San Diego. Harry and me sold cars, used cars. At that time I was beginnin' to fix here and there again.

I used to sneak off to Tia Juana sometimes and get a fix. One time, the Mexican secret service police stopped me. I gave them some money, and they let me go. Another time they stopped me. I didn't have no money. They put me in jail and took the car away. My friend Harry bailed me out.

It was a big mistake, though, callin' Harry. The Mexican police found out I had friends with influence. They figure, "Oh, we can make some money off this guy."

This is junk drivin' me; I come back again and the same secret service policeman stops me. I tell him I haven't got no money but I'll get him some. He says, "All right now—I'll give you a half hour."

So, you know what I do? I burn him—and he's the chief. I didn't burn just any guy, I burned the chief. He said, "If you don't come back, I'm going to tell you one thing—don't *never* come back." I said, "I'll come back. Don't worry. I got it covered."

And I don't go to Mexico again for a long time. But then the urge gets me again. If I try to score in San Diego, the narcotics agents are goin' to know about me. They will find out about me. That's just the way it is. I don't want no static in San Diego. At the same time I want to get some better stuff and it's only a forty-five-minute drive to Tia Juana. So I take that chance again.

I didn't take a car this time. I went on a bus. What actually happened was the connection fingered me. Just when I'm off the bus, ready to cross the line . . . wham! They smash me.

I said to myself, oh, man. I know I'm in trouble now. I've got a couple of hundred dollars and I tried to buy him off. He ain't listening. He's sayin', "Take this no good son of a bitch out of here."

By this time, I've been around long enough to know that I'm in for bad trouble. They put me through the wall. They call it the disappearing wall. There's a wall, but it opens some kind of way. This is the headquarters of the secret service police. They shove you in there and nobody knows. So I'm back behind that wall, I know I'm in for trouble. And nobody can help me. That's when I start saying, "God, help me. I need help, help me, man."

Guys die in that room, man, guys get killed in there; tortured. I know this. I seen it. And now I'm in it. Inside the place. I'd rather be in any joint—Joliet, Folsom—any joint in the states but there. Give me all the time you want over here but don't put me in that little room. I know I'm in trouble.

I see two or three other guys being wasted. I'm telling God now, "Just let me take what they're going to give me. Don't let me say anything." I've got so much on my mind about what happened that I could incriminate a lot of people, plus myself. So I'm asking God, don't let me open my mouth, let me take this. That's all I'm asking. But I know I'm in trouble.

They work on another guy. They make me watch, and they are accomplishing what they wanted. Getting me scared. But then, they made a mistake. On weekends, the FBI comes to check on the American sailors that are in the tank, to get a report. This was Saturday and they had a lot of sailors from San Diego. They let the FBI see me in this little room. That was their mistake.

They got me charged with rape, murder, and stealing. They had me held there on account of this eagle, this tattoo I got. The guy that did these things had an eagle on his arm. He got blonde hair, he weighs a hundred and eighty pounds—but he had an eagle. I'm dark, a hundred and fifty. He was five ten, I'm five six. You understand? So it didn't mesh, you know.

What happens is that these big guys who are holding me split for the weekend. I had been talking to the sailors who were in there. I became friendly with some of them. So when the FBI came, these guys told them something about me. I wasn't on the list, you know. The FBI man—he was a Spanish guy—he said, give me the other man that's in there. They said, "There's nobody in there." He said it again. I hear all this. So the FBI man said he'd go see the chief. "He's a U. S. citizen—I've got to see that man. What you got him here for?" They gave him the charges. He knows what's going on. He said, "I don't want nothing to happen to this man." If something happened he said he would take it to the chief, the chief of the whole shebang, the Ocalde.

The Mexican police thought I knew all the tricks of the trade. One of the policemen said, "Not too many guys go in that room and escape. You the first one I've seen. I congratulate you. I want to buy you supper." And he did buy me supper, man. These are hard guys, man. The Mexican police are somethin' else. They're mean. And this guy, he said,

"Well you did this, you know, but that will never happen again."

Then I came back to Texas, that's when I was goin' to the pen as the outside sponsor. I read in the paper about James Allen. The article said there was goin' to be an expert talkin' on the subject of drugs, at the Christian Reform Church. So I went to see Mr. James Allen. I told him who I am, showed him my tracks.

I expected the guy to preach, and he don't preach. He just knows about drugs. He runs it down. I wanted him to go to the joint with me and talk to the guys.

At this time, I'm not fixin'; I'm sincere. Mr. Allen says he can't make it but he says I should come around the ARC when I'm in New York.

Two months later I'm usin' stuff again. I called him collect and tell him I want to come but I don't have no money. He said, "If you are fixin' man, you'd better not come—unless you have intentions of stopping." I said, "That's why I'm callin'. I don't want to be this way."

This is the truth, man. I'm not jivin'. I got to tell you this, because we addicts do lie. See, I know I got a good comeback chance, 'cause I'm with the Bible. I'm goin' religious. Maybe it don't look like it, but I'm a very religious cat.

Now I feel that all the money that's passed through my hands, all the opportunities I had, maybe it isn't all lost . . . I might still have a wonderful chance. I could have been a politician in Mexico or a big businessman in Texas—that's not just talkin', you know. I had chances but I always put myself in a mess. So I don't feel bad, you see, because I have the chance to make a comeback. Not too many guys have that.

On March 4, 1968, after a year in the ARC program, Pancho's urine analysis came back with "codeine, heroin" next to his name.

IKE

". . . Where was I?" The new Ike hangs up the phone. "Oh yeah. So I read up about the law. And I knew a little about psychology. If the judge turned his head or looked up at the ceiling, I stopped. 'Your Honor, I would like to have your attention.' Now, I know that he doesn't really have to listen to me. All he has to do is say, 'Do you have anything to say?' I say three words and he can say that's enough. I've had my say as far as he's concerned. But I would make my opening statement such that he will be willing to listen on. In one case I remember, the arrest was right; I had heroin but the officer stuck his hand in my pocket without a warrant, which is also against the law. When the case comes to court, the two plainclothesmen say that I threw the heroin down and they observed me throwing it down. When it comes right down to it, they goin' to believe the policeman's story, not mine. Right? There's no point me gettin' in front of the judge and sayin', 'Your Honor, I didn't throw no dope down.' He ain't goin' to pay me no mind. So I have another story.

"I've been up all night, burnin' matches in the cell, makin' sure I have my story memorized. When the judge says, 'Do you have anything to say before we pass sentence?' I says, 'Yes, Your Honor.' I had pleaded guilty to a misdemeanor, 3305, possession of drugs. I can get a pen bit—one to three years—for it. I know this, of course, and I'm trying to duck this one to three years thing. So I says:

" 'Your Honor, unfortunately I wish that what has occurred to me would have occurred twenty years ago. Then I probably wouldn't be standing here now. Because I was under the impression that two wrongs do not make a right.' " Ike straightens the knot on his tie and holds his head up like a substantial taxpayer. He clears his throat and continues. " 'But, apparently the court feels that two wrongs *do* make a right. It was wrong for me to have the drugs in my possession but I also feel it was wrong for the police officer to take them out of my pocket' . . . The judge gave me six months.

"You know why? Look, he knew I'd have enough sense to put in a writ and if I did and it went to the Appellate Division, I could beat it, see. For the simple grounds that when the police grabbed me and put me in the hallway, they did it so roughly that a patrolman on the street runs after us with his pistol. See, he don't know who these two guys are; they're dressed shabby as I am. You dig?

"They pull out their badges and say, 'Police officers, we're police officers.' The cop says, 'Oh, okay. Everything all right?' They say, 'Yeah, yeah—we're police officers.' And I saw the patrolman take out his booklet and look up at the house number and make a notation. I popped off his badge number. So he could be my witness because they didn't say nothing about the hallway; they just wrote me up that I threw it down in the street.

"I told this to the Legal Aid, I said, 'Look, if I get jammed, I'm goin' to put a writ in. And after I put my writ in, I'm goin' to put in a "show cause" forty-eight hours later.' So they gave me six months. There's really no point me putting a writ in because by the time it goes through, four months will be up and then with red tape I'll have to do the six months anyway."

The first day in the Center, Ike tore his only pair of pants on a sprung spring. Ike was very bugged, cursed a lot and felt that itch. An old friend, already in the program, told him, "Man, I know you gonna cut this place loose. You ain't goin' to make it."

Ike formulated a plan. Math had been his best subject in school, one reason he'd been so good at taking numbers. He applied mathematics again, figuring: "It averages me about six months from the time I get on the street till the time I get strung out, arrested, and locked up. I'm going to give myself six months, but instead of doin' wrong, I'm goin' to do right this time. When the six months are up, I'm going to see what I've got for my six months, whether it's been worth it or not."

Ike doesn't live in the house. Being a free spirit, he says it would be a bit "confining." He doesn't want anyone telling him to be in by twelve o'clock. As it is, he's usually in his apartment by ten thirty, at work every morning at nine, has three bank books, a library card, and he voted last year for the first time.

Hired to be on staff at ARC after four months in the program, he started another six-month plan. A few months later, he was moved up to a more responsible job—the reception desk—and renewed it once more.

There is nothing about him, except his job, which tips off the past. His teeth are still good. There are no visible needle marks and he looks much younger than forty-four. You wouldn't guess he just became a grandfather. Walking to the subway, past the Silver Rail bar ("2 for 1"), the Irroy Hotel ("Radio in every room, $3.75 a night"), the Thomas Bar-B-Q, the Sunset Theater ("3 Big Features")—closed—past easy-credit furniture stores, the Baby Grand Club, meat stores advertising chitlins cheap, Ike looks like a schoolteacher or an Urban League official in his new tweed topcoat.

"Problems that you have I laugh at. For instance, you might get your paycheck and say, 'Oh, man, they took so and so many taxes on me.' But when I get my check, that's the least thing on my mind. I *know* they gonna take that, so that ain't nothin'. That's not even my money. I don't mean you in particular, I mean like the average person—you know, squares. They complain about taxes goin' up. I know the taxes are goin' up, and so, that's nothin'. If I go to the store and I say gimme a pair of shoes I don't think of what I paid twenty-five years ago for the shoes. The man say, 'A good pair of shoes they cost twenty-three dollars.' I say, 'So what? I know that.' I'm not expectin' to go to the store and get a good pair of shoes for twelve dollars. So the small things like that, you know, they don't even worry me. I know everything's sky high. I accept this like it's normal because I've lived such a life that the things that squares complain about, I laugh at.

"I got a square brother. He works for Con Edison. I say to him, 'You got any money in the bank?'

"He say, 'Huh?'

"He's always leaving ten dollars in the bar every Friday night. That's silly. Before I'd leave ten dollars in a bar over here, I'd rather go down to the Copacabana and really have me a pleasant, enjoyable evening. Who knows, I might meet a rich widow. I'm not goin' to meet a rich widow down the corner in one of these juice joints, although either way is a horrible way to spend it.

"My brother doesn't have one credit account. All he has is his workin' clothes. Really. He's young, about thirty. I just mention him in comparison. Like I asked him, 'What political club do you belong to?'

"He say, 'Huh?'

"I say, 'Brother, do you have any money in growth stocks?'

"He say, 'Huh?'

"Me, I can't wait till I can afford me some growth stocks."

The new Ike jogs across 125th Street whistling "Without a Song."

From *New Life* (ARC newsletter):

TO:

Mr. & Mrs. N.Y.C. Junkie:

I am sure that for years and years you felt that no one seemed to care if you lived or died. You have been branded by the marks you carry on your body, as just another junkie, just another no good greasy worthless junkie. Well . . . NOW at last in 1967, N. Y. State has at last begun to think about you, if you think anything about yourself . . . Don't you really feel it is about time you began to think about yourself and your future. From the first day that you realized that you were addicted to drugs, you have spent all that time thinking about someone else. (In case you don't dig it I'll tell you whom you have been thinking about)

You have thought about someone to . . . ROB . . . CHEAT . . . CON . . . SELL DOPE TO . . . OR TRICK WITH . . . YOU ABOUT THE PERSON YOU WERE GOING TO COP FROM. . . . (HOPING YOU WOULDN'T GET BURNED) YOU THOUGHT ABOUT THE PERSON WHO BAGGED THE STUFF (HOPING YOU WOULD GET A GOOD BAG) YOU EVEN THOUGHT ABOUT THE STOOL PIGEON. (HOPING HE OR SHE WOULD

SPARE YOU) BABY . . . YOU THOUGHT ABOUT ALL THESE PEOPLE BEFORE YOU THOUGHT ABOUT . . . YOURSELF. YOU ALSO THOUGHT ABOUT THE POLICEMAN WHO MIGHT CATCH YOU AND LOCK YOU UP (HOPING YOU MIGHT OUTRUN HIM OR OUT THINK HIM, AND GET AWAY) YOU EVEN THOUGHT ABOUT THE D.A. THAT MIGHT NOT GIVE YOU A MISDEMEANOR (HOPING THAT HE WOULD) YOU THOUGHT ABOUT THE LAWYER, WANTING HIM TO GET YOUR FREEDOM (HOPING THAT HE COULD)

YOU THOUGHT ABOUT THESE PEOPLE AND MANY, MANY MORE: YOU HAVE WANTED SO MANY PEOPLE TO THINK ABOUT YOU . . . WHILE YOU HAVE STOPPED THINKING ABOUT . . . YOURSELF . . . THAT BAG THAT YOU COPPED . . . IT COULD HAVE BEEN ANYTHING (INCLUDING POISON) THAT NEEDLE THAT YOU USED, IT COULD HAVE BEEN INFECTED . . . THAT POLICEMAN COULD HAVE SHOT AND KILLED YOU OR PARALYZED YOU FOR LIFE . . . THAT TRICK COULD HAVE BEEN A*%##&¢$&& MANIAC . . .

Maybe you have been lucky. Just think of ALL the junkies who have not been as lucky as you. You are lucky because you have in your grasp a chance at "A NEW LIFE"

At the MANHATTAN CHRISTIAN REFORMED CHURCH, ADDICTS REHABILITATION CENTER, under the Direction of Mr.

James Allen and his entire staff you can receive:

Withdrawal hospitalization . . . Group Therapy . . . Job Placement . . . A chance to return to school . . . Religious conselling . . . educational counseling . . . and a great deal of understanding and compassion.

There are many, many more activities to help you abstain from the use of drugs, if you would just take the time and the interest to visit our Rehabilitation Center, which is located at 253 West 123 Street. At the Center you will see things, with your own eyes and hear things with your own ears, then you will find out first hand that we at the Center do care about you . . . if you care about yourself. The ARC is open from 8:00 AM-12 Midnight.

VISIT OUR CENTER AND REMEMBER THE LIFE THAT YOU SAVE COULD VERY WELL BE YOUR OWN AND THE NEW LIFE YOU BEGIN WILL BE YOUR OWN. . . .

IKE HOUSTON

3
Just About Out

A ragged man, just about out in a doorway, manages to raise himself on one elbow and waves a sorry attempt at a nonchalant greeting.

"Hey . . . my man . . . How'ya doin'?" James Allen waves back. Without breaking his short, determined stride, he says, almost to himself, "Why don't you get up from there? That's no position for a man to be in."

The man drops his back to the stoop and a few seconds later is fully zonked-out once more.

Seventh Avenue jumps uptown. The sidewalks swing with men smiling, slapping each other on the back, hugging. These men are different from other Americans—more like Greeks, Italians, or perhaps Arabs. They do not feel their masculinity threatened by a physical display of affection for each other. The streets in Harlem serve the same purpose as cafes in Paris. People live much of their lives in them—and for the same reason. Apartments are small, too cold or hot inversely to the season, uncomfortable; good to be out of.

In suburbia, men mow their lawns, trim hedges, wash their cars, or chat over split-rail fences on the weekends. During the week they are somewhere else. In Harlem there they are every day; standing by lampposts, in doorways, in front of bars and soul food joints.

There's one now—smoking a long cigar on a top step; just digging the scene, looks like, wearing a sharp, light brown camel's hair coat and a fedora to match. Maybe he works at night, or weekends. What can a black man do to be so idle and dressed that well? At any rate, he is not using his leisure time creatively.

Another is washing his car between two stripped wrecks, among garbage. It is a brand new American car and he seems very fond of it. There is something weird about a man washing his brand new car parked in garbage on a weekday.

On the fashionable East Side, during a business day, one sees well-dressed women, some with shopping bags, nannies escorting kids and dogs, delivery boys, chauffeurs. On Seventh Avenue and 122nd Street, there are men, lots of men. A group of seven passes around a jug near a place called "LIQUOR." They have been there a long time—forever, it seems. A big yellow car double parks. Somebody takes the bottle over to the driver who swigs from it. Two prowl cars cruise by, one after the other. The police don't look twice at the scene. It's not unusual.

In front of James Allen's house, a bunch of kids are playing with a dolly, pushing it around, laughing. "Boy, we could use that thing at the Center," he says. "I wonder where those kids found it . . . hey, you kids. . . ."

Allen's apartment in the Manhattan Christian Reformed Church building is clean and uncluttered—only a few chairs, a cheap couch, a portable television on a wire stand, no rug. Under a dime-store color photograph of John and Jacqueline Kennedy there is a second-hand spinet. And, a guitar case in a corner.

"Mary . . . Mary." No answer. "She must be out. My schedule is pretty hard on her. She's never sure when I'll be home—I'm not exactly regular. I guess she's gotten used to it though. Mary's a good woman. I promised to take her to a movie tonight. Don't think I've seen one in six months.

"Hey . . . what do you think of this piano?" He opens the keyboard. I play a few chords. All the keys work.

"It's funny how I got it. Wanna hear?" Allen, like so many

ex-junkies, is one extreme instead of the other. After years of nodding out, of being enervated, they explode somehow when junk leaves. They become insatiably horny, can't stop eating, or talk incessantly.

Allen talks: "One day last summer I decided to get me a new guitar, so I went down to Forty-Eighth Street, where all those music stores are. You have to realize, Mike, that I had the cash in my pocket. I wanted to buy this thing, you know. I was coming right from the Center and I had this here junkie jacket on. . . ."

"A what kind of jacket?"

"This basketball jacket I have on now, and jeans. I guess I was pretty ratty, but the salesman got me mad anyway. He wouldn't pay me any mind. He kept watching me and every time I picked a guitar to try, you know, he would come over and take it away, saying something like, 'You couldn't afford it anyway.'

"You know, I think he should have given me the benefit of the doubt. Anyway, boy, I was mad! So, you know what I did? I went down the block to another place and bought this piano. I was meanin' to get it for my daughter anyway. Then I went back into the store and waved the receipt at this guy; two hundred dollars' deposit, all cash. Mike, you should have seen the look on his face."

Allen's head is shaved. What little fuzz there is peeks through in irregular patches. He rubs it and laughs. "Would you like a soda or some coffee? Sorry we don't have anything stronger."

"You don't drink at all?"

"Not really, although sometimes Mary and I have a glass of Manischewitz with dinner. I guess we've just gotten out of the habit. And I have to set an example for the guys."

He stops on the way to the kitchen. "You know, I love what I do, although I've always harbored in the back of my mind this thought that I would like to be a guitar player. Maybe that's silly, but I see how bad some of these guys are on television. I guess I'll always have that fantasy. But my work is very creative. I think so. It's kind of like—I'm creating human beings, creating clean man days. It's satisfying."

A woman, her hair in curlers, appears behind him.

"Oh, hi Mary. Where were you? I called a couple of times."

"I was in the bathroom." She smiles with embarrassment. Allen introduces us. She looks at him with mild disapproval. "I didn't know anyone was with you."

"Oh, it's only Mike," Allen says. "Why don't you bring some coffee, baby?" He kisses her on the cheek. She is taller and heavier than he is; not beautiful; a good-humored, strong, handsome woman. She goes for the coffee.

". . . I'm not trying to turn out an army to fight against drug addiction. I am trying to turn out an army to fight against community conditions whatever they may be; the pissing on the streets, the whole bit. I'm trying to put these people in a position where they become aware that these things exist because we allow them and that the least we can do in order to eliminate some of the wine-drinking on the street is not to drink ourselves. This has a contagious influence upon the community. Ofttimes winos will at least turn away and hide it from me now. I mean this. I get this sort of thing when I walk down the street and it's amusing.

"You see, I'm a dope fiend. This is my street. I shot dope here. But now when I walk down the street, I notice people won't put in their numbers in front of me. They know damn well I'm not going to tell the police but they respect my attempt to live decent and normal in the community. You understand what I mean? And it's not that I'm such a great fellow. They're just looking at what I'm doing. This is the kind of spirit I'm trying to instill in the people who come through the Center and will go back out in the community.

"Last night a guy came over to see me. He met a girl when they were both in the program and they got married. He's been on the street over a year now and he's kept the same job that long. Last night was the first time I've seen him in six months. First thing he did was whip his bankbook on me. He showed me there were no withdrawals in six months. It's a positive habit. This guy hadn't worked since 1957. ARC got him a job and he's been on that job ever since."

Mary brings the coffee on a tray, her curlers covered with a kerchief. She leaves us right away.

Allen forgets to say thank you. ". . . And it was a terrific adjustment for this guy because he doesn't have any particular ability. When he was in the program we thought about sending him to school but sometimes the challenge of going to school can be detrimental to a common laborer. Everybody can't go up there. For them it is best to get in a situation where they feel comfortable. This is the object of our program: not to force a person into something that *we* think is good for him, but to assist him into a situation that's comfortable for him."

Allen makes $8,500 a year. He pays no rent. His car is free. He lives in the middle of his ghetto, spends all of his time with dope fiends and has, despite himself, become a member of the Establishment. He seems comfortable in the role, a man with a purpose, a calling, a sense of himself. It wasn't always so.

Born one of five poor kids in Grand Prairie, Texas, he grew up mostly on his grandparents' farm near Ringgold, Louisiana. He hated that farm, it was like a penitentiary. His parents separated. In high school, Allen was too small to play football. He scrimmaged anyway; one minute in his senior year. Along with everybody else on the team, he got an athletic scholarship from Southern University. It was a good year for Ringgold, but he went to Los Angeles seeking freedom instead.

He found only the ghetto, the black glob existing in what the North defines as freedom. He was lonely and lost, just hanging out. A guy around had a beat-up guitar and Allen plucked on it whenever he could.

"Hey Mike; I finally bought that new guitar last week. Wanna see it?" He takes it out, tunes it and asks: "You know 'Yesterday'?"

I play it on the piano. My version has all sorts of dissonances worked out late one bitter night, when I could neither write nor sleep. We are not at all together and just manage to get through it.

"I'd better learn it," he says. "I'm supposed to sing at a church social tomorrow afternoon."

In L. A., Allen wasn't on the church social scene. He slept in basements and back yards. He hung around the Lincoln Theatre, in the ghetto, and began thinking of a show-biz career as he fetched coffee and ran this errand and that for the people working there. Only this is not a James Brown/Ray Charles success story. Nobody discovered him.

He drank with the guys and smoked pot whenever possible. On pot, Allen thought he sang better. He smoked and drank more than he sang. Any kind of high interested him, any time.

A year later, back in Louisiana shining shoes, he was good and strung out. He learned to press clothes. He bought a guitar and gave up the pressing business. With another guy, who played a tub-drum, he supported himself from bar to bar on tips. They both had conchs.

After that, he was in and out of jail, traveling from Louisiana to Georgia, stealing, back to Louisiana and finally to New York City leading the same bullshit existence. Harlem is the inevitable destination for a black American junkie: Harlem is where the action is.

Somehow he got married which didn't last long. His old lady soon tired of his habits and copped his key to their apartment one day. He could come back when he was clean, she said.

He decided to get even: he would clean up and come back in a big Cadillac car and everything—then tell her to fuck off. He'd ride all over her. Allen volunteered into Lexington where he found himself just another derelict. All the others there scared him. What was he doing with his life? It became clear that he was, after all, no bigshot. His old grandfather was nothing but a poor sharecropper, farming with a mule on land he didn't own, and even he had more peace of mind.

Feeling stupid about it, he got on his knees one night and tried to pray. He prayed again, meditated, read the Bible. But could even Christ have faced Harlem sober?

From *New Life* (ARC newsletter):

THE FICKLE MASTER

The Addicts Rehabilitation Center is housed in the heart of Harlem, in a place where the buildings seem to bear witness to the innumerable tragedies that have left their scars on the sidewalks. The Addicts Rehabilitation Center stands there looking down on the city and through the bright lights that stream from its glassy eyes, a ray of hope is found.

Hundreds of souless men and women wander through these streets in desparate lonliness and hardly a sound could be heard above the roar of a busy city. Faceless, nameless, prideless creatures dancing to the tune of a master that won't take no for an answer, his music of temptation seems sweet and gentle, offering some forbidden sensation. One can hear his voice in the darkness of the mind saying "come with me child of the dark, forgotten soul, come with me lonely and impoverished heart and I will be bread for you, come with me, discard, and I will whirl you away from this world that drinks your blood and then asks for your flesh. Come with me and I will take your worries and cast them into a sea of forgetfullness come with men and dwell in a fantasy where every day is filled with joy and like the pied piper, the rat infested population dances merrily after its master."

And the only clear voice that can be heard among the clanking doors of hospitals and the silent sounds of needles is a slender intense man and his staff in an upper room that looks down on the merry go round of the addict and says, "come impoverished and find a glimer of hope come lonely one and you'll find people who care about you, come aimless and find direction, come desparate and find dedication, come pridless and find self respect. Forget the master. I was once his slave. Be not afraid for I have overcome and so can you. Give me your dejected, deserted, disillusioned and discontented bodies, bring your minds, bring your problems, bring your ambitions and let us try to give you what we have forgotten."

The battle still rages, hundreds still suffer, the master still calls and thousands hear his voice and follow, only to be left strung out in the street all over the world. For the master is a fickle lover who lives off broken lives and frustrations of a decadent society. He has no respect for person of position. Everyday he leaves you longing to hold him and have him carress you in his arms of forgetfulness. He's out there now calling, but if you just listen you will hear the voice of the dedicated saying, "look to the staff of the Addicts Rehabilitation Center and take the first step. Look up and begin to live again."

New Life

4
Why Bill Glenn?

A group of seven or eight of us all started at the same time. It wasn't a club or a gang or anything, just some guys who used to hang together. And I'm the only one that's alive.

I didn't do any less than the others, but in all those sixteen years I used drugs, I never even had a serious cold. I ask the question, "Why me?"

Once, my friend and I needed a fix badly. We were very, very sick. Oh, we needed drugs *very* badly. We were at the point of passing out—both of us—by the time we stole some money, went to cop the drugs and got a cab home. He was in such a hurry that he figured, "Oh well, I'll take a snort."

Not me. I wasn't going to waste any drugs on a snort. I was going to wait until we got home, fix properly, and get really straight. It would only be another few minutes.

"I can't wait, I can't wait," the guy said. So, when the cab stopped for a red light, he opened the bag, quickly tore a piece off a match cover, and took a nice big sniff up each nostril. Within seconds, blood started gushing from his nose and mouth. He was dead before the light changed. He had snorted pure lye. He couldn't wait. The connection had never dreamed that a confirmed dope fiend would ever try to sniff the stuff. In the normal course of events, it wouldn't have happened.

Anyway, I got out. I ran. I opened that cab door and kept running. There was a piece in the paper about it. I imagine they were looking for the other guy; me. At the time I didn't give it a second thought.

There was another time, the day before Thanksgiving. Two of us were sitting around my house cooking-up out of the same bag. I always had extra sets of works around; they were always ready for use. So he had one and I had one.

We drew the shot into the dropper and put the needle in our arms. But for some reason my needle clogged. The stuff wouldn't go in. So I had to take it out again and clean the needle. In the meantime he went on, he used his.

I see he's sitting there, going into a very deep nod and I'm saying to myself, "Oh this is very good, this is very good stuff." I'm sick and I'm trying to hurry and I'm very annoyed because this sort of thing never happens to me and I need a shot badly.

He keels over on the floor and I'm thinking it's very good stuff. Oh, man, this guy is really high. I'm hurrying, trying to clean the works out. Then I hear this rattling sound. I've heard that many times: the death rattle. I put my stuff down—still haven't used it—and look. This guy was in convulsions. I picked him up and tried to give him a salt shot. But he just died. Inside of twenty minutes he was dead. It was a hot shot—the stuff was no good. The drugs were mixed with rat poison or something. A lot of pushers sell these things to guys they think are stool pigeons.

That needle had been in my arm. I was in the process. I think that was the first time a needle had clogged on me. And this guy's dead.

Incidents like this have been happening all through the years of my addiction. At one time another guy and I were both sleeping on roofs, in basements, standing in the cold without enough clothes, hanging out together for quite some time. One day, we were walking down Eighth Avenue—up here on a Hundred Forty-Fifth Street—looking for a way to buy some drugs. He just fell over, he fell dead. He had walking pneumonia. And there I was walking along just as healthy as could be.

Why me? Why am I the one who always comes out on top? There I was doing everything in my power to destroy myself and yet nothing happened to me. Now I can see these were warnings, but at the time it never occurred to me.

I never questioned anything. I just figured I was lucky. I wouldn't take heed. It just seemed a natural course of events. I became a burglar; that's how I kept my habit up. Something happened I still don't believe. I was a derelict; dirty, sweaty, sick, like a wild man. I was way up in the Bronx, in a middle-class neighborhood where, if you got into an apartment, you could be pretty sure of finding something of value: a ring, a watch, or a small radio—something you could put in your pocket and pawn.

I knocked on the door. I rang the bell. I listened. I was positive that if anybody was sleeping, I had made enough noise to waken them. At these times, if somebody came to the door, I would always say that the superintendent sent me. There's something to be fixed. Isn't this apartment so and so? Of course it would be the wrong apartment and I'd get the hell out of there.

Well, anyway this time nobody answered the door. It was very quiet. I listened. I didn't hear any movements inside. I even got down on my knees and tried to look under the door to see if there were any shadows, anybody walking in their stockinged feet.

I went up to the roof. Most of these old houses have dumbwaiters. They haven't been used in years. I'd learned ways of telling which shaft goes to which apartment and I opened the shaft and went down on the rope.

Now most of these ropes haven't been used in ten, fifteen years. They are so rotted a fly would be a little reluctant to climb down one. But I never gave it any thought. Once you start falling down those dumbwaiter shafts, there's no way to stop; the slightest snap and you are finished. But I never so much as started to slip and I did it a hundred times.

I climbed down the rope with the twelve-inch crowbar I always carried to open the sealed doors. I pushed, broke the plaster, opened the door and stepped down. Naturally this is the kitchen.

The first thing I saw, just in front of me on a table, was a woman's purse. It was very fat. Near it was some change and a dollar bill. As I walked over to it, I heard just one word: "Freeze!" And I froze, believe me.

The voice said, "All right, turn around—real slow."

I turned very slowly. My hands were up. I saw this big fellow, a young fellow, in his twenties. He looked like a giant football player. He was pointing a gun at me.

"Drop that crowbar," he said.

I dropped the crowbar.

"Come over here," he said. "Sit down."

I walked over very slowly and he kept his distance. I was shaking, sick. I needed a fix.

He picked up the phone and dialed with one hand, still pointing the gun at me with the other. He called the police station and said, "Hello, this is patrolman so and so." I've forgotten his name.

Now imagine that. He's a police officer. I was burglarizing a cop's house. He didn't hit me. He didn't even say a harsh word to me. The patrol car came with two other cops, he put on his uniform and we all went over to the precinct.

After they found out who I was and what I'd done, the other cops started calling him all kinds of names. He was a young fellow, probably on the force six months or so. They were telling him, "You big so and so, you big dodo. . . ." Actually they used much stronger language. "You caught this no good junkie bastard breaking into your house? I would have killed the bastard. You should have emptied your gun into him. You would have been promoted to detective. You would have gotten the five-hundred-dollar *Daily News* award," which is true; heroism in the line of duty. ". . . Breaking in your own house? You should have shot him! What do you care? Kill him. One more junkie out of the way."

This is what the other cops and detectives told him. He didn't even answer, he was just sitting there asking my name and typing me up on his report. Then he took my fingerprints and whatnot, took me inside and locked me up. The only thing he said was, "Here kid. . . ." He's calling me kid—I'm probably twice his age. ". . . You'll probably need to buy some cigarettes." And he gave me five dollars.

Wow! I mean . . . You know? . . . I looked at him. I didn't understand the real essence of what had happened. I was very sick from drugs.

The next morning they sent me to the tombs to await arraignment. That night, as I was laying in the cell, a voice came to me. Honestly! A voice came to me and said, "This is the last warning." I heard it quite plainly: "This is your last warning."

Out loud I said, "What do you mean, my last warning?" The word "warning" made me think back to all the warnings before. Here eight of you started out, hundreds of other addicts have died for various reasons, more have ended up with serious illnesses, and you are still alive, healthy, with all of your mental faculties.

Then the voice said, "The next time that you use some drugs, the gun is going off." And then it dawned on me. I became so frightened. I began perspiring. Fear gripped me. I felt that bullet going into me. I understand it now. A perfect set-up. I'm breaking into a cop's house. He was in his pajamas. He and his mother live there alone. He would have only been protecting his own mother. He had every legitimate reason in the world to kill me: not just shoot, kill me. I looked like a maniac. I had a weapon which, believe me, I would have used without the slightest qualms. If I'd had the opportunity I would have hit him with that crowbar; I didn't want to go to jail.

He must have known this, yet he gave me nothing but kindness and consideration. There are over twenty thousand policemen in New York City and this was probably the only cop who would not have shot me. And then he winds up giving me money out of his own pocket. All of these things hit me at once.

In court, he came to prosecute. He was also the arresting officer. He went back to the bullpen where I was standing and called me over. By this time he knew my name. "Bill, come over here," he said. "Don't worry, I'll do everything in my power to make it easy for you."

I thought, "What is this guy . . . some kind of nut?" I burglarized his house and here he is doing everything in his power to help me.

He said, "I'm not going to press any charges. I've got to tell what happened but I am going to recommend that they take it easy on you. Don't worry too much. Do you have anything to smoke?"

I said no. He asked the guard, "Is it okay if I give these to this guy?" I remember so well because they were Kools and I don't like Kools. The guard said, "Okay, yeah—go ahead," and he gave me the cigarettes.

When we went into court, sure enough he made it seem as if nothing had happened. Because of his testimony, the charge was only unlawful entry, which is really nothing. If my record wasn't already so bad I would have only received thirty days. As I was led away, he looked at me as if to say, "I'm sorry for it." I don't think I'd recognize him now, though. I wish I could remember his name.

That was the first time I ever thought about God. Honestly. I was brought up to respect God and Christ but I never really paid any mind to it. I didn't become a religious fanatic by any means, but I began getting some help from the Bible. And I began to suspect that God had been saving me for some purpose, although I didn't know what, at the time.

When I came in here, I saw what Allen was trying to do. He was staying off drugs. I saw all of these addicts coming in wanting to be helped. I saw all the help they needed.

Then it hit me. This is where you belong. This is what you were saved for.

5
Your Blue-Eyed Boy

The first time I kissed Paula she went all the way. She was like that. We were lovers for a few months. Three nights a week she came; tall, tawny, eighteen. A sophomore at the University of Miami, I lived off campus in a one-room garage apartment.

In my part of Coral Gables, simple C.B.S. houses hide comfortably behind heavy tropical foliage. A large, sweet sea grape hung over my door, which was open for the breeze. Night creatures were deafening. Jasmine and bougainvillea interlaced with the sweet odor of marijuana; "gage," as we called it then.

We stayed in bed all evening; smoking, listening to Vivaldi, making love. A drive-in at midnight for barbeque beef sandwiches and milkshakes, then home to her mother's.

Pot was essential. "Anything that can make you hungry, horny, and sleepy has got to be healthy," we said.

We were an orgy three nights a week, moving to the Mass in B Minor, to the rhythm of crickets, to the rustling of leaves when there was wind; slowly, long, together.

These days there is talk of dropping out. Paula was before the term. Nothing was important to her; politics, religion, family—not even sex really. Her orgasm was a quiet "uh." She never smiled balling; only stared at the ceiling or the wall. Once, I was angry about something she'd done and yelled at her. She cried, which surprised me. I hadn't thought I could touch her that way.

The magic decreased with winter. She began working at

the dog track and we could have only her night off, an occasional afternoon or late night together. She made friends at the track; touts, mutuel men, bartenders, musicians—people who drank, gambled and partied to all hours.

Paula and Dolores—who worked next to her—soon became best friends; drinking beer every afternoon and hard liquor at night when someone else was paying. Some thought they were making it together.

One night, Paula, Dolores, and a beach boy named Sal were turning on in Sal's convertible. Having trouble deciding what to do, they just drove around. The moon was full. They parked on a dead-end by the bay, smoked some more, and listened to Machito over radio Havana. It was an aimless night, neither unpleasant nor unusual.

Along Indian Creek Drive, Dolores remembered a dyke who lived nearby. The dyke had heroin and wanted to trade some of it for pot in order to get close to some freaky girl, the wife of a doctor. They fell by. Dolores and Sal had fixed once before and could hardly wait. Paula just stuck out her arm like everybody else, not wanting them to know it was her first time.

Occasionally I'd run into Paula on the beach, in some saloon. She was friendly but distant. We had nothing to say to each other. Paula was after something I couldn't give her.

Soon she was seen with a drummer named Danny, who made her pregnant shortly before moving to Las Vegas. Her first abortionist scraped her womb unnecessarily three times, after which she had constant pain for months and was never quite the same.

She spent a muggy summer sitting in front of a fan at Dolores's place. In bra and panties, her hair pinned off her neck, feet propped on Dolores's wicker table, Paula sat it out reading novels all day and half the night. Dolores had a connection and, when the track reopened, Paula was ambulatory and they both had screaming habits.

When Danny called her to join him in Vegas, she took the next Greyhound without a thought. She might be in love with Danny. To stretch her supply of dope, Paula bought paregoric during rest stops.

By the time she reached Vegas, however, she was out and could only think of one thing. Without enjoyment, she let Danny do it to her. That long, dumb trip for love and all she wanted was a fix. It was then she realized what she was.

Paula was a reader; novels, philosophy, mysteries, history, anything. (She read *War and Peace* on the bus.) Now she began with the available literature on addiction, soon learning that it was not heroin she was hooked on but opiates in general, that there was no reason to be sick as long as a drugstore was open.

A year later, I met her in Coral Gables. I could see she had changed and knew why; she was not my only friend with a habit. She had lost a good deal of weight and I noticed the scars on her arms.

Over coffee at Whalen's, our conversation was tangential, punctuated by awkward silence. I leafed through the book on opiate addiction she was reading. Passages were underlined. One of them gave three qualifications for an addict. First you must know what you are taking; if it happens in a hospital after a sickness you may be safe. Second is knowing that a lack of dope makes you sick. Third, take drugs just once to cure that sickness.

I offered her a ride home. At a traffic light we somehow kissed and ended up at my place again. When she stripped, I saw her breasts had shrunk pitifully and there were tracks on her thighs. I couldn't make it.

Taking her back—she was once more living with her

mother—we were silent. She asked me to drive to North Miami, way out of the way, to a drugstore she knew. When I finally dropped her, she kissed me lightly on the cheek.

Paula's mother goes to Temple. She lives modestly on an annuity, spending her time and energy on Hadassah work. Mrs. Gross knew something was wrong with her daughter but not what. Instinct led her to search for strange objects around the house.

"I think you should see a doctor, Paula dear," she said one morning.

"Oh come on, Mother. I'm not sick."

"Why do you fall asleep so much then? And you are always dropping your cigarette—you smoke too much anyway."

"Mother, I wish you would cut it out. Nag, nag, nag. I'm just tired from work, that's all." Paula acted fed up.

One morning Mrs. Gross was cleaning the bathroom. She saw a strange jacket on the hook. There was a set of works in a pocket, although she didn't know what it was. She confronted Paula.

"That's Boots's jacket. I borrowed it from her last night. Remember how cold it was?" She examined the works as if for the first time. "I wonder what it is," Paula said.

"Paula, you are lying. I know you too well. Please tell me; what is it you are doing? I would like to help you. Maybe you should go see Rabbi Goldstein."

Storming out of the house, genuinely hurt, Paula couldn't understand how her own mother could call her a liar.

Dolores and Paula spent a lot of time in the bathroom. After reading an article about dope addiction in *Reader's Digest,* Mrs. Gross began to suspect and really worry. She searched more carefully. Behind the hamper, in a small crack down by the hinges, she found a little packet of white powder. Paula said she had never seen it before.

"Paula, you are taking some kind of dope, aren't you?"

Paula screamed, "Mother you are getting senile. There is nothing wrong with me some peace and quiet wouldn't cure. Why do you keep after me all the fucking time?"

Mrs. Gross was born in Russia, came to Buffalo at the age of twelve with her parents, who went into remnants there. She married a window salesman and eventually moved to Miami because of her husband's health. They were a close family until Mr. Gross died of a heart attack five years ago.

She knew absolutely nothing about drug abuse. When Paula insisted that people who drink can't take dope, she believed it. She was almost happy Paula drank so much. But that week, Mrs. Gross had three long conversations with Rabbi Goldstein.

One night Paula didn't come home, which wasn't so unusual. Mrs. Gross had resigned herself to it. This time, however, as she was leaving for synagogue, the mailman delivered a special delivery letter. Paula wrote that she had left town, that she had stolen some checks and forged her mother's signature. In addition, she had taken an insurance refund check and cashed that too. The total came to over nine hundred dollars. She apologized and hoped her mother could forgive her. "You were right, Mother dear, I am an addict. I think you will be happier without me around. I am so sorry. I love you."

Mrs. Gross was hysterical and Rabbi Goldstein had to go with her to the bank. It seems that Paula had come with the checks, saying her mother was ill. The teller, who knew the family, cashed them—although the forgeries were quite obvious. The bank offered to make good. But they would also have to call the FBI into the case; their insurance obligated them. Mrs. Gross would not permit that.

Paula couldn't hook. She wasn't the type. She was too thin anyway by now. Besides she always managed to hold down a job in some office or other. Her experience with business machines at the dog track got her a part-time job with a small insurance agency in Atlanta, where she got off the bus.

Not knowing where the junk was, being too shy and lazy to look for it, she settled for the drugstore once more; there is almost a quarter grain of morphine in a bottle of paregoric. She knew how hard PG was on the stomach, and it gave no flash, but it kept her reasonably straight. At times she would switch to cough syrup. Paula stayed that way in Atlanta over five months. She had another abortion there.

Fresh drugstores became scarcer and she started taking more risks. After one proprietor threatened to call the police because she had been back three days running, she called home, saying she wanted to be through with dope, even believing it herself. Mrs. Gross was extremely relieved to hear she was not in jail or dead, and agreed. Paula could come home "until you can get on your feet again."

Paula found a job, another insurance agency, and Dr. Breuer, both within a week.

Dr. Breuer was a nice old German who felt sorry for dope fiends. He wrote papers and gave lectures about addiction and the mistake it was to treat it as a crime and not a disease. Everybody came to him saying they wanted to kick and he was easily conned, writing liberal prescriptions "for curing drug addiction." Being sincere didn't make this legal in Florida. It also didn't change the fact that Dr. Breuer was, in reality, more a connection than a doctor.

Junkies are marvelous con men; experts at begging for sympathy because they are so pitiful and sick. Catering to them does not help the cure. Looking for an easy way out, for pity, for instant gratification, the inability to cope with so-called reality, are the symptoms which led them to dope in the first place. Dr. Breuer, like so many well-meaning professional squares, was a sucker, accomplishing nothing.

Eventually the state narcotics people caught up with him and he barely stayed out of jail. But while Dr. Breuer maintained his "cure" program, Paula spent much of her free time in his waiting room, which was usually packed with happy, expectant junkies.

Dolores was hooking for her habit. Unlike Paula, she was not ready to settle for drugstore highs. One summer night when there was absolutely no dope in town—Miami is seasonal for connections also—she decided to break into a drugstore for some heavy stuff. Paula went along. The alarm sounded and they were both busted for the first time, after three and a half years.

Rabbi Goldstein used his influence with some prominent politicians in town and managed to keep it out of the papers. He also arranged for Paula to go to Lexington—rather than the women's reformatory—where she spent an enjoyable three months cleaning up, reading, and listening to the good jazz band which played almost every night. Sober was high after three and a half years; a kick.

Not much is known about what Paula did after her release from Lexington. Even Mrs. Gross lost touch. Apparently she lived, at least part of the time, on the beach, ran around with beach hustlers and struck up a close relationship with a Canadian pharmacist for a while.

Then there was Carlos, a hustling Cuban bartender who pushed junk on the side. Carlos grew up in the slums of Havana. He was a hard drinker, wise in the ways of night people. Despite a prodigious temper, Carlos gave a good deal of softness to Paula. They moved in together. A part of Carlos wanted children and a calmer life but he absolutely refused to be poor again. When he settled down, it would be on his own terms. In the meantime he earned a hundred fifty a week, stole another hundred from the register and sold heroin.

Charlie Parker died two days after Carlos and Paula were

married. Bird had been Paula's role model; an intellectual junkie, a junkie by choice, not circumstance—so Paula thought—an addict in the tradition of Poe and Baudelaire. There was so much in his head and the world was so unreceptive. He stayed out of it because of his superiority. Bird could never shuck. He always played as he lived; flat-out, with no thought of tomorrow.

According to the obituary, the attending doctor estimated Bird's age as fifty, fifteen too many. Although there is nothing about her marriage in the diary she kept sporadically, there are a few pages about Charlie Parker, ending with a quotation from e.e. cummings: ". . . and what I want to know is how do you like your blue-eyed boy Mr. Death."

Carlos was not a user. He was hot-blooded and soon began resenting Paula, who became increasingly less responsive in bed. Basically the monogamous type, Carlos was not satisfied by the beach whores he occasionally took to hotel rooms. He lectured Paula about dope, beat on her at times, and threatened to cut off her supply.

"You are getting to sound just like my goddam mother," Paula said to him. "Man, the trouble with you is you don't really understand me. Maybe you should take off once. Why don't you? How can you have the nerve to come on to me about junk when you've never even made it yourself?"

Carlos thought it might help at that. He felt strong enough to control it.

One shot a week soon became two a day. He rationalized that he was drinking less and it was certainly helping his marriage. They were home more, together most of the time now, like a regular couple. He liked tieing up together, helping each other in the ritual. They had something in common now, kind of like a baby.

This baby cried a lot: four times a day. "He would have made it sooner or later anyway," Paula thought, which was probably true. Besides, they were in good shape. Carlos had money and junk and money and junk together is no problem. Rich junkies live to ripe ages; eating well, being sure of their vitamins, sleeping enough, using clean spikes, taking fewer risks with the law.

One night, Carlos was hanging out with another barman he'd seen around. "Man, do you know where I can get a little schmeck?" the guy asked him.

"I don't know," Carlos said. "I'll ask around. Come by tomorrow." Carlos checked him out, discovering he worked the early shift at the Roney Plaza. He had been there all season. He seemed okay. Carlos sold him two bags, which was a mistake because the guy was the Man. It cost him five to ten.

It has been sixteen years since I knew Paula. Until this book I'd almost forgotten her. I called Miami information and found Mrs. Gross still listed. Not knowing whether I'd be remembered, or my call welcome, I hesitated several weeks before making it.

Mrs. Gross recalled me vaguely. Paula was dead. Yes, she would be glad to talk to me about her; "Maybe it will help other children," she said.

I flew down. A dark-skinned child, about seven, greeted me at the door. "What's your name?" she asked with a slight lisp. "Nanny says you knew my mommy." The resemblance was clear; those same almond eyes and almost orange hair.

"Yes, I knew her. She was beautiful like you. My name's Mike, what's yours?"

"Nanny . . . Nanny, there's a man here to see you," she skipped into the kitchen. Mrs. Gross was about as I'd remembered her; we all age together. She showed me into her Florida room. The child jumped on her lap.

"Linda, why don't you go out and play," she said. "This gentleman and I have to talk."

"My name's Linda," Linda said, grabbing a cookie.

"After you called, I looked through the garage and found this," Mrs. Gross said. "I thought you might like to read it."

Paula's diary; her handwriting is often illegible, always sloppy and tends to run off the page.

July 10th. Last night we broke into a drugstore. It seemed silly not to take the money too. Bruce knew there was no burglar alarm because he works for the company that is supposed to install it next week. (Ha ha on the burglar alarm company.) He used a glass cutter. We found two bottles of morphine and plenty of dollies. A hundred and ten dollars too.

August 3rd. I guess I have an irresistible touch of larceny. Besides, I feel it is my duty in a way to steal from insurance companies. They are always so pleased when they sell some poor "sensible" jerk a policy he usually doesn't need. The salesmen talk about making a "good deal." I hate those salesmen with their stupid cracker accents.

I feel like Robin Hood stealing from them. Or maybe Lenin. I supposed I am a closet communist. Always the outlaw. I just can't resist—whenever I see a system of some kind, I automatically start figuring a way to break it.

September 28th. Whoops!!! Busted. And for only $158. They were nice about it, I must say . . . wouldn't have been if they'd known about the other six thousand I've swung with so far. They said they knew anybody could have a lapse and I've been such a good employee—if I paid it back there would be no trouble. Of course they would have to let me go . . . of course. Those jerks, they just deducted it from my back vacation pay. I cried. Oh, what got into me? I needed the money for an operation. I threw myself on their mercy. I had been so happy working there too. I confessed. Better get out now, before they begin checking other things.

December 12th. No shit in town. Last week I had to ride the bus for two hours down to Kendall to find a new drugstore. Maybe I'd better kick . . . Oh God, I hate that.

December 14th. Bruce brought me saggies last night. I took twenty-four of them—twenty-four. Isn't that incredible? And on top of two bottles of PG. I never closed my eyes for one minute. I just lay there moaning. Just think, twenty-four pills and I still couldn't sleep. That would kill two normal people but my nerves are still screaming. With other kinds of pain you will usually black out when it gets bad enough, but not kicking. It's a nervous pain, a direct attack on your nerves. I feel like a dentist has been drilling on my teeth for three days. If only I could get some shit. . . .

January 26th. It's nice having a *little* habit again. Really nice. It's a great feeling to only need so little. Of course it can't stay this way, but right now I don't have that horror hanging over me.

February 9th. Dolores just got out. How wonderful! She looks so well. I wonder for how long. Not long, I imagine. Our life is such that jail is a place to get healthy.

February 12th. Dolores, Bruce, and I shot up some paregoric last night. Bruce does it all the time. Cooking PG is such a big deal—fun though. Dolores and I have always thought it is such a shame that you have to burn the alcohol out of PG when you shoot it. We'd rather have the alcohol too. And it's a nasty process; if the works slip out of your vein, the pain can be excruciating. You want to go through the ceiling. I'd almost rather drink it.

February 14th. I think I would have been at any rate an alcoholic. I've always been a heavy drinker. For Carlos, drinking was a way of life. Funny how little I think of him. He'd have to have a drink before he brushed his teeth in the morning. Carlos was a sick person as far as drinking was concerned.

August 8th. My baby was born with a small habit. The doctors say she will live.

August 22nd. Carlos was paroled last month. He wrote to me. Mother told him about Linda. He wants to adopt her, but first he will get a job. He sounds happy.

Mrs. Gross told me that Carlos had learned the trade of barbering in prison. But, when he applied for a license, the authorities in Tallahassee told him ex-cons were ineligible. Carlos stayed straight selling cemetery lots for a while, bell-hopping at night during the season. He'd spend almost every Sunday with Linda, taking her to the zoo, the beach, or the circus when it was in town. After a while he came around less frequently and then not at all.

Mrs. Gross looked so small by her front door. "You know, it's funny," she said. "Just before Paula died, I read an article in *Life Magazine* about that place for addicts in California. If I had only known about it earlier, I certainly would have seen to it that Paula went there."

She apparently hadn't read the final entry in Paula's diary: ". . . Old-timers like me really shouldn't even try to stop. Maybe earlier, but now I wouldn't waste my time thinking about it. Dope is as much a part of my life as eating. Face it Paula, you are nothing but a broken-down junkie."

6

Laundromats and the Sober Republic

News filtered back east about a place called Synanon, on the Santa Monica beach, supposedly run by a bunch of ex-addicts. Zev Putterman, an upper-middle-class Jewish junkie, considered it probably another nutty southern California fad. Zev knew that an ex-addict was a rare beast.

Frankie Starvo and Rita Cohen were rumored to have squared up in Synanon. If true, that was incredible news because they were both badly strung out for many years. Zev became interested, but he had just about enough energy to make it to the Bronx for his connection, let alone California.

Zev was tired of cures anyway. He had had them all: the Menninger Clinic in Topeka, the Institute of Living in Hartford, three times in Lexington, The Holbrook Sanatorium, The Westport Sanatorium. When he heard of the British system of legal maintenance for addicts, Zev sailed the next week on the *Queen Mary*. When Mrs. Marie Nyswander began her research program with methadone, a non-escalating, heroin-blocking drug, Zev was on that scene too. For fourteen years as a junkie, he went through them all.

His father was Rabbi of the Park Avenue Synagogue and Zev rattled around between his images: WASP Park Avenue, Judaism, and junkies. He liked being with musicians, painters, and writers, being the center of attraction around talented people who normally played that role. He was bright and witty enough to pull it off.

Zev was a great storyteller, a spellbinder. Sometimes he

made speeches on behalf of State of Israel bonds and other such causes. In his Brooks Brothers clothes, Zev was a successful fund raiser, high out of his head.

One night, WBAI, an FM station, played some tapes of Chuck Dederich, Synanon's founder, telling his story. He scared Zev off even further, talking in his teutonic, autocratic way. What could be worse than a teutonic ex-lush from Toledo, Ohio? No. Zev preferred to press on in New York, as always.

Over the next year there were more rumors about Synanon, more of the old crowd supposedly cleaned up. Then he read the spread in *Life*. It was a cold, windy day in March. Zev was sipping a coffee with other junkies in Joe's and got to thinking about the sunny Santa Monica beach, all those broads in bikinis.

He gathered a variety of pills and substances, spent an afternoon at Brooks Brothers, wound up miscellaneous business and split.

No broads in bikinis at the East Harlem Protestant Parish, only Reverend Norman Eddy and ten or twelve dope fiends sitting among urban garbage. Someone told James Allen about the goings-on in the old storefront on East 100th Street and he began to make the pilgrimage twice a week when his career—washing dishes, pressing pants, bus-boying—allowed.

For a while he was situated out in one of those quaint old revolutionary inns we white folks like so much. Some nights he slept out there, in the New Jersey hills. He took long walks in the morning. On a clear day he could see the towers of the George Washington Bridge, which made him want a shot of dope every time.

Reverend Eddy's little program was all Puerto Rican. Allen always thought they were discussing him in Spanish. He was uneasy there, off balance. He searched for a church in central

Harlem, eventually turning up at the Manhattan Christian Reformed missionary center where Reverend Eugene Callender was stationed, working with the natives in the jungle.

Callender was holding meetings with addicts every Monday night. Allen made those, plus Sunday and Thursday over at Eddy's place. During the day, he pressed clothes. On Sunday he went to church. He did a lot of praying all the time. Still clean . . . day by day.

With Teddy Richardson, another guy staying off, he began performing a little skit around town: for B'nai B'rith groups, women's clubs, church groups, and so on. The idea was to reach people who, if they became interested, could change things. The skit went something like this.

First a little pantomime about how people get hooked. Then a volunteer from the audience is asked to play the role of a minister. Allen plays the addict.

"How are you, Reverend Smith? You don't know me because I'm only a young man. But I used to be a parishioner in your church—in fact my mother is one of your heavy contributors. I'm a drug addict and I need some help. I thought I'd come to you because you're a man of God and you say God loves us. What can you do for me to help me kick my habit?"

The volunteer was all of a sudden put in the position of trying to provide some assistance—and there was none available in New York City. The only thing he could do was recommend Lexington, and that took about six weeks to get in. The skit was left hanging with "Well, thank you Reverend. If I'm still alive by then, I'll come back when you get the papers from Lexington."

The plague was spreading. The New York Council on Drug Addiction was formed. It included Callender's missionary station, Eddy's little program, the Quaker Friends, some doctors and social workers. Callender assigned one of his staff of four, Miss Tona Kenbeck, to work part-time coordinating their narcotics program with the Council. But she got married and the program fell apart. When Callender was transferred, the new minister, Gordon Negen (the missionary station had become a full-fledged church), asked Allen if he would like to continue in her place. The job would pay seventy-eight dollars a week plus a free apartment. He stopped pressing clothes.

As many as a hundred addicts a week passed through. He talked to doctors, nurses, politicians—turning the pressure on. Some doctors began prescribing Doriden, Coricidin, Ridylin and Thorazine. At that point addicts came not to rehabilitate, not to program: just to ease some pain. Allen took them to a doctor, had them examined, chaperoned them to a drugstore. There didn't seem to be any law against it. After a while, druggists who knew Allen gave him medication without a prescription. They knew he was okay, and there was so much pain.

Church groups began getting work for some of the guys. Volume doubled almost immediately. After kicking, addicts started coming back a second time looking for work. The meetings—just bull sessions really—became more frequent and crowded with guys sitting around the church, talking about addiction, trying to stay off.

At the beginning, Allen felt rather guilty in his new role. It wasn't like work; pressing clothes, chauffeuring, waiting on tables—*doing* something. It was his first desk job and it took awhile for the droves to come. He found himself sitting around the office with nothing to do. Killing time, he practiced typing, studied a little Spanish. If a guy would come in who knew some algebra, he'd algebra him to death. Same thing with chess and Ping-Pong.

More and more came, guys making it out there by themselves—day by day, one more clean day at a time. Some had jobs, some were on Welfare. They needed company. It's impossible to hang tough like that all alone for long. They were reluctant to leave at night and closing time grew later.

Organization was loose but growing. Turned-around junkie cunning conned food, old clothes, furniture, and games from the community. Some cooked, some cleaned up. Everybody did his bit.

One rainy Wednesday Josh was making it down 122nd Street with a monkey on his back, not going anywhere in particular. He saw the church door open, which is rare on a weekday in Harlem. Generally the representatives of God stay away from that flock when they can help it. Josh was curious; and wet. He came out of the rain, met Allen who soon talked him into the hospital. Josh started working around the place for a dollar a day plus room and board. He was a professional cook. Meals became more regular and tasty.

By the winter of 1961, the Manhattan Christian Reformed Church was housing about twelve addicts in various stages of rehabilitation. Hundreds of other guys passed through every week, mostly for a free meal, some warmth and company, and a little compassion. But one would have to stretch the definition to call it a program.

Then came a mysterious shipment of five hundred pairs of "hush puppies" from somewhere in Michigan, followed by dope fiends looking for shoes. Getting rid of them increased volume even further past capacity.

The momentum picked up more when the Eastern Deaconal Conference, a New Jersey church group, started contributing $170 a month.

After the Metcalf-Volker Bill had been passed by the New York State Legislature, Metropolitan General Hospital opened a small ward for detoxifying addicts. Now Manhattan General joined in. Allen had gone to Metropolitan hoping to work out an arrangement for referring addicts there. Maybe he wasn't well known enough, maybe he had his junkie jacket on, or maybe they just didn't think he was stable enough—at any rate nothing came of it.

He went to Manhattan General with the same idea. Mr. Brooks, in charge of social services, was amenable. Miss Bowles, in charge of admissions, said okay too. They would accept his addicts for treatment and send them back to him afterwards without red tape.

It worked. Others were beginning similar things with other hospitals. Addict rehabilitation was becoming a popular business. Everybody had his own plan, his pet peeves and theories. Should ex-addicts or professionals be in charge? Should a guy kick cold turkey or by gradual withdrawal? There were particularly strong feelings pro and con about the methadone maintenance program.

But more or less everybody agreed that if a guy could be detoxified and get a job, he could make it with the help of a day-care program vaguely analogous to Alcoholics Anonymous. Nobody even dared to admit to himself or anybody else that something formal, another step like a halfway house was the real answer. The idea was too unreal: impossible.

All this time Allen had suffered, strangely enough, practically no static from the precinct house around the corner. Once, a patrolman had staked himself out in their hallway, keeping tabs on something or other in the street. Allen told him to leave; the cop was scaring the customers away. He later regretted that—the guy was just doing his job—but Allen hadn't quite come to the point in his own rehabilitation where he considered the police his protectors. Now he says he does.

Other than that, about the only hassle was because the cops parked their cars in front of the church and Allen could never find a place for his own.

At the same time, Synanon was fairing less well with the law. The Santa Monica *Evening Outlook* published editorials about the "undesirables" in their community. Good citizens became concerned over the dope fiends in their midst. The Establishment acted. After all sorts of legal maneuvers, Chuck Dederich was locked up for twenty-five days, charged with violating the zoning laws. Before the cell door clanged behind him, he said to a friend: "For many years I tore up and down the highways drunk, endangering my own and other people's lives, without serving a day of jail time. Now that I'm in the business of attempting to help people, the community locks me up. Maybe on a deep level, some people don't want addicts to quit shooting dope."

Synanon looked for another place, finally deciding on a spot zoned for agricultural use in nearby Malibu. More hysteria there. People talked about buying police dogs to protect their wives and children. The lawyers and commissioners went at it in defense of the sober Republic, despite the fact that Synanon had not even been accused of one illegal act—other than zoning—in the four years of its existence. It remained in Santa Monica.

Flying out, Zev knew one thing for sure—a drug addict is someone who has taken his first cure and then goes back to it. The cure becomes part of the addiction process. Synanon would be no different. They must be using drugs in there. Drug addicts use drugs. He wasn't terribly optimistic but he was tired and he'd tried everything else. Early in the morning, just off the plane from New York, he received a cold welcome. "Sit down and shut up," they told him. All the other places had greeted him with the "good-to-have-you-aboard" number, but there was an idiot at this reception desk. Obviously he didn't know Zev had just arrived in California and that he knew a Synanon board member. A continent from his connection though, and still high, he sat down and shut up.

They copped his bags. One of them chock with psychic energizers, tranquilizers, and sleeping pills which his psychiatrist had prescribed for poor Park-Avenue Putterman. Then he waited. Outside, on the beach, there were no broads in bikinis. It was raining, as a matter of fact.

At the intake interview they told him he'd never make it, he was spoiled, a compulsive talker, unable to learn anything, probably incurable. Six guys were at Zev. When he tried to answer, they told him to shut up. "Man, what do you know? You're a junkie. What can you teach anybody? You've got nothing to say. Look. There's thirty-seven years of sobriety and eighty-two years of addiction here, so your fourteen years of addiction and three seconds of sobriety don't count."

They talked about him as if he wasn't there. "Let's take him downstairs, let's do this or that to him. . . ." He wasn't consulted. The main thing that had appealed to Zev about Synanon was that there weren't going to be any "we" and "they" alienations, "because these are folks like me, and they know how sick I am." Something was wrong.

He was taken downstairs by a guy who looked like a cop and it looked like a precinct house there. The guy poured all Zev's pills down the toilet. Zev said, "Now wait; you don't understand, these are non-addicting drugs. They're legitimate. I have a prescription. See, my name is on the bottle." The guy went on pouring.

Zev had produced and directed a number of plays in New York. He had his eight-by-ten glossies with him. They were important, his identity. In show business, your pictures, programs, and clips are what you are. These were all taken from him, and rudely, along with his clothes and substances. He asked for a cotton shirt from the commissary, saying he was allergic to wool. They gave him a wool shirt, which didn't fit. The rest of the official issue was clean but definitely not Brooks Brothers.

His luggage was gone, his résumés, his identity, his drugs, his pride. Also his hair, by way of a square barber, much squarer than the one he'd had the day before at Vincent of the Plaza.

Zev was getting sick. "I'm not feeling very good," he said.

"You will not get any medication," they told him.

"You don't understand. I'm going to be really sick. You see, I'm from New York, and they've got good dope in New York, and I'm really going to get sick."

They said he could always go back to the good dope in New York.

Candy Latson started the therapy. Zev was sweating and retching. "Little Brother," Candy said, "when are you going to get sick?" Zev was flipping—Candy's attitude was ridiculous—but he decided not to give the big spade the pleasure of seeing him sick.

Coming on that way, Candy let Zev know that he knew that Zev knew that he knew. There is a deep understanding that an addict communicates to another. In every other institution Zev had gone through, it was we and they. Because of his background, Zev had been even further split. He was kind of like "them," but because of some fluke "they" became doctors and he was a dope fiend. His soul was with the dope fiends; he knew where "we" was at, because the doctors didn't know where *anything* was at.

At Synanon there were a million manifestations of himself. There were many different types in there—different colors, ages, backgrounds, and educational levels. They had only one thing in common. One strong and ugly thing. It was ruining their lives.

Candy knew how to handle Zev because he *was* Zev. The we-they thing which had been between Zev and his father, his psychiatrist, and all the doctors and wardens he had ever known didn't exist. The place was populated by a hundred faces of Zev. His sense of alienation—the hip and the square, culture and subculture, in and out group, Jew and Gentile, white and black—was beginning to be destroyed.

Candy watched him kick cold turkey, which Synanon insists on and which isn't all that bad; like a super-rotten cold. Every morning, Candy would come over to him and ask, "Hey, Little Brother, when are you going to get sick?" Zev had no intention of giving him the satisfaction.

Immediately Candy had destroyed the unconscious symptoms a kicking junkie uses to get approval, sympathy, and a fix. There was plenty of nausea and diarrhea of course, but after four days Zev was beginning to function again. He had become an expert at kicking from observing himself so many times. He had even read Cocteau on the subject. Now, all his theories were destroyed by the fact that he had a good night's sleep on the seventh night. He hadn't slept so soundly, in or out of an institution, in many years.

As a reward, he was handed a mop, which dragged him to put it mildly. He felt he rather deserved some kind of a prize. Instead, he was told, "People don't shoot dope. Therefore not shooting dope is not worthy of a reward. You don't get a reward for not beating your wife."

Zev was a lousy mopper. They told him so. He became increasingly sure he was just a piece of worthless shit. For years he'd stolen, cheated, conned, and lied. Now he was mopping floors, which was just what he deserved—and he couldn't even do *that* right.

In square institutions for dope fiends, guilt is catered to. "You can't help it. You're sick. Poor guy. But don't worry, we'll work this thing out together. You'll see." Junkies love that.

In Synanon, if Zev didn't mop a corner clean enough, he was told that the dirty corner was like a corner of his own soul. Instead of catering to Zev's guilt, they fueled it, made it unbearable, impossible to forget. And if a transgression was serious enough, Zev would get another haircut. A shaved head, they feel, is an inescapable reminder of guilt.

After a while, Zev began to notice that if he mopped well, even if it was in a corner nobody checked out, he didn't feel quite so guilty. He almost began to like mopping. Besides, he wasn't going to mop forever. He began to learn something other than instant gratification. In his thirties, Zev was finally beginning to grow up.

In Harlem, even after growing up, a man is still a "boy" and may very well continue mopping floors forever. Allen firmly believes in "different strokes for different blokes." Spade cats get "haircuts" all their lives. Why ram more abuse into them? When a guy says he wants to kick, Allen gets him in the hospital fast and then worries about motivation. An addict isn't capable of any positive motivation as long as he's high—once off, a spade junkie is not generally motivated by anything more noble than fear and weariness. He becomes tired; tired of running and hustling, tired of going to jail, being hungry, sleeping on rooftops; afraid of an overdose and an early death.

By 1962 addicts were really jamming the Manhattan Christian Reformed Church program, sleeping in hallways, on floors and benches. It was a stockade—a defense against the Man—pusher, cop. Getting high just didn't seem to make sense anymore, but what else is there? Maybe if we can all be together, cry together, then maybe.

It was a scene from Hieronymous Bosch, the orgy in Viridiana, an African leper colony. The contagion could not be contained in the street. Some men nodded out sitting in the pews. Others drank wine. Jazz was played on the church organ. The hush puppies had disappeared, boosted and fenced fast by certain elements among the passing parade. Allen and his few volunteers had no money, no formal program and insufficient personnel. They could not police the scene. All of this did not appeal to some of the less imaginative officials in the church hierarchy. The program seemed stalled.

"We just couldn't keep up with it, you know." Allen finishes his fourth cup of coffee and bums a cigarette. The apartment is overheated, but I am sweating as much from the story. "It was the weirdest thing . . . cigarette butts were all over the church floor. When the guy from the state came in, the addict on piano switched from 'Night in Tunisia' to a hymn. Very funny."

The New York State Department of Mental Hygiene was prepared to give him money. All they wanted was a proposal. But two years earlier, Allen had written one which went around to some public agencies, all of whom rejected it. He had also written an article for *Harper's Magazine,* at the request of one of their editors, and it too had been rejected.

"You know, it was like writing a song which nobody wanted. Why write another one? So we just ignored the Mental Hygiene people. I guess they finally sent this guy down out of exasperation. He came on a good day too . . . he kept saying, 'Look, we can give you up to a hundred twenty-five thousand dollars for an operational budget. Just submit a proposal.'

"I'm sitting in that little two-by-four office with addicts all around me and I've never owned anything. You understand? That much money was really beyond my concept of thinking. I kept telling him, 'Well, you know . . . that much money, I wouldn't know what to do with it. I'd feel like a damn fool sitting around here trying to spend a hundred twenty-five thousand dollars. Just leave me alone.'

"What he told me then was, 'You can use some of it to rent a place.' But, you know, I just wasn't in the mood for doing any more writing. You can't imagine the frustration I had gone through with that *Harper's* article. So I made excuse after excuse. Finally, he said to me, 'Look, we'll loan you a consultant to write it,' and I said okay.

"Their man came and spent a whole week showing me how to do this and what to ask for. He still couldn't get me to ask for any more than thirty-five thousand. They finally sort of twisted my arm and gave me forty-eight thousand anyway."

Allen rented a loft on Eighth Avenue between 122nd and 123rd Streets and hired a bunch of guys who had been off drugs for a while, many of whom left better-paying jobs. Others continued chauffeuring, running elevators, cleaning up—those things black people do in America—working with the program part-time, solidifying their own rehabilitation while counseling others. Rich Feimster, a non-addict college graduate experienced in church and social work, came in as second in command. And so the "program" became a Program.

It is getting late. Allen has been talking for hours. It is too late for the movies. Mary went to bed long ago. This is my first day up here and it has been a long one. I have a headache. The back of my neck cracks when I turn. I feel the need of a shave. My hands are dirty, my spirit low. I have been hearing so many sad, sad songs.

Call me Mr. Pitiful,
Baby that's my name . . . ooh
Call me Mr. Pitiful,
That's how I got my fame.
But people just don't understand now
What makes a man feel so blue,
Oooh, they call me Mr. Pitiful . . .

Otis Redding was not singing about these men who have nodded through their adult lives. But he knew them, and he might have been. Now they are trying to adjust to so-called normal society, the white society which wants nothing they have other than passivity and invisibility. They are not interested in staying clean because junk is bad. Junk isn't "bad." It's good. Junk works. It eases pain. Junk is stupid, that's all. The dues are too heavy.

Allen's job is his life. There is no separation, no days, nights, weekdays, or holidays. No business or pleasure. No let-up. He is not yet finished: "I tell you quite honestly, Mike, I was determined that I was going to take this agency and build it up on experience, not on window dressing.

"I've always been involved in my own program and I've made certain to keep myself free of strings that would structure me into some sort of procedure that comes out of somebody else's mind—somebody else who has never slept on a rooftop. You understand what I mean? My thinking is that if these people could be all that effective in narcotics rehabilitation, they would have had the problem solved while I was still out there sticking a needle into my arm. It is clear that they don't know what is to be done and I don't care how many degrees they have, they are not in a position to dictate an effective approach. Maybe they can learn—I'm sure some can and will—but they haven't proven it yet.

"It's very basic. It is a fact that an ex-addict, attempting to relate to an active addict, is able to understand those little thin lines between his honesty and dishonesty. For example, where other programs, publicly funded and operated, were using urine testing, out of necessity, we don't need it. We don't need a urine test to tell when a dude is high. We may use it to document a situation for the sake of others, but we use it sparingly. Sometimes we confront a person and we can't bring him to the point of admittance—then we'll use it, as a last resort.

"Now what has happened is that Governor Rockefeller . . . and I'll say this quite honestly. I don't know whether he's a good governor or not because I don't know anything about government, but he's the only governor I know of who has been able to appropriate this much money to try and help the addict. Now the thing I like more than anything else is that the state program is willing to give my agency and others an opportunity to prove our effectiveness. Before this program came into being, the only way you could really get any funds anywhere else was if you knew somebody. You don't have to know anybody to get the state money. All you have to know is your job. So far, anyway, it seems to be a program that funds programs on their merit, their ability alone."

All day long Allen and his assistants have been telling me about their program and others, each with its own particular theory about how addicts can be rehabilitated, about the growing competition between them for public funds. It is fast becoming an industry, and addicts rehabilitation centers are almost as easy to find in New York City as laundromats.

I have been shown budgets and brochures, facts and figures about cures. I have been told sad tales. All of it is rattling around in my head illogically. How much of it was a con? Synanon methadone NACC Daytop Exodus House James Allen Phoenix House SPAN David Daitch Dr. Efram Ramirez OCAP AWARE RARE . . . There is so much to learn.

Part Two

THE HOUSE

7
In Defense of Opera

Saturday therapy sessions are for residents only—no day-care people. They are scheduled from ten till two. Mr. James Allen presides.

Things started slowly, somewhat late—not unusual at ARC. Although I had been around the house for the better part of a week, and knew most of the guys—at least by name—Allen introduced me formally: "I'll tell you just like it is. You remember when that article was in *The New York Times*? Well, I got a call from Prentice-Hall—a very pleasant female. She expressed an interest to have a book written. I figured she was some old hag, you know, but I made an appointment with her and she came up. Well, it turned out to be a very beautiful young lady. She talked about the book. I didn't hear anything she said—but I agreed to everything. As a result, she writes me a letter saying, 'All right, we'll do it.' In the last line she says, 'We'll get a writer.' I got a little shaky but figured maybe she'd send another beautiful young lady . . . and she sent this horrible looking guy."

Everybody looked at me, not all of them smiling. Mine was the only white face there, except for Pancho, who is Mexican and rather dark anyway. The chairs were in a semicircle around Allen, at the reception desk near the front door. I was in a corner, inconspicuous I hoped, my theory being that there are times a reporter should blend in with the bushes. I smiled and waved, nonchalant as possible.

"But I was in so deep by then I couldn't do anything. So what is going to happen is that a part of the royalties will be contributed to the program. I don't get anything personally. So that is what he's here for, to get an idea of our program. Okay?

"Now let's get down to business, just like he isn't here. . . . Anybody got a screwdriver?"

The fish tank pump was making an awful lot of noise. Allen tried to fix it. Everybody rapped in the meantime, drinking coffee and bumming cigarettes. The informality was just about reaching the point of chaos when Allen gave up, calling them to order. Scheduled to start at ten, the meeting finally began in earnest at eleven.

Nix complained that the day room was not being cleaned properly. "Someone should be assigned the job," he suggested.

"Now wait a minute. . . ." Allen was getting in gear. "Why wait for someone to assign you. You ought to get together and decide who will do it among yourselves. . . ." Three or four guys spoke together, shaking their heads in disapproval. ". . . Hold it. Hold it . . . just a minute. You ought to do this just like you do your own cleaning chores—on a rotating basis. Then you free yourself of having Mr. Randolph tell you to do this or that. You get what I mean?"

In his late forties, Mr. Randolph is about five feet tall, compact and in excellent shape. Calm, impassive, he has a private telephone line in his private room upstairs, which he keeps immaculate. He rarely goes out. Most of the $2,400 a year the Center pays him as Residence Manager goes toward clothes; his suits are custom-made and he buys forty-dollar shoes. Mr. Randolph put a cigarette in a holder when his name was mentioned.

". . . This is a rule that you shouldn't have to have imposed on you. You are asking us, in essence, to assign you the job of doing this. Now this is not at all compatible with learning how to function out in society."

"In other words," Nix said, "we should get a list together and submit it for approval."

"Yes, uh-huh." Allen paused momentarily, wrinkling his brow. "You should all get together and decide on the list. See . . . I'm trying to save you the trouble of having some staff member tell you to do something you should have done six months ago."

"It won't work." Nix is always wearing a hat, or holding one. He is a bulky man with some teeth missing in front. His clothes are on the ratty side. Nix has only been detoxified a few months and often dances to the soul music in the day room. He is always complaining of some ailment. "No sir, it won't work," he repeated categorically.

"Well," Allen said to him, "nothing is going to work if you go into it with a negative attitude. This is what kept us all shooting dope so long: because we had a negative attitude about life. As long as you think something won't work, it can't work. And you will do little things to keep it from working. I mean that. This goes for all of you. It will work. All you got to do is do it. It will work."

"What about a television set?" Nix is a study in paranoia. "We need a television set. Last week you said something about not getting one unless we buy it. Speaking for myself, I can't. . . ."

"Oh, come on Nix. I never said that. We got at least four stacked around here. They can be repaired. I said that I wouldn't *buy* one, but I never said we wouldn't get one."

"What do you mean you won't buy one? You mean personally?"

"I mean the program won't buy one. We can't afford to buy equipment. Get it? But there are a thousand ways of getting a TV without buying one—or boosting one. How did we get the records? They were given to us. Right? How did we get the TVs that we got? They can be fixed. What's the difference if it is new or old, as long as it works?"

"Come on man, let's be practical," Lindy said. "Let's get one repaired now and then worry about a new one when the program has the money." Lindy Stokes is tall, lean, very black. His short hair has quite a bit of gray in it. Lindy shot dope with James Allen years ago and has been in the ARC program for a year. Although something of a clown, always putting people gently on, his eyes are quite sad. Lindy is always shaking his head with an "I-don't-know-what's-the-matter-with-you-guys" smile. "But we do need a cartridge. The record player doesn't work either."

"How much does a cartridge cost, Lindy?"

"About twenty dollars, sir." One hears a lot of "sirs" and "misters" around ARC.

"The program can buy a cartridge. But then what you have to do is make sure that every Tom, Dick, and Harry doesn't use the machine and break it right away. You should assign maybe three people in the resident program to be responsible for the record player."

"That's right," Lindy said. "But I think that it might be better if everybody contributes to the cartridge, rather than the program buying it. Speaking for myself, I can afford a dollar or two. That way we can make sure it is treated right. If you have something personal involved, you will take better care of it. You will be surprised how you will abuse someone else's things. But you will definitely protect your own. Definitely."

Nix was secretary of the meeting, sitting next to Allen taking notes. He kept calling for a resolution but everybody talked at once while Allen was downstairs seeing about the heat. One is always overheated around junkies. Detoxified or not, they can never seem to get warm enough.

Lindy made a motion that the guys chip in for the cartridge and designate three people to be responsible. The motion was carried.

Nix looked up from his minutes. "I'd like to say something. I'm still confused about the difference between 'free time' and a 'pass.' "

"You want to explain that, Rich?" Allen turned to Feimster.

Rich Feimster has the build of a linebacker, the face of a reverend. He is second in command, heading up the day-care after-care portion of the program. His main posture seems to be striding firmly from room to room on some sort of urgent business, holding a sheaf of papers or a clipboard. He leans forward in his chair, furrowing his brow. "Free time involves certain geographical limitations. It was developed, actually, for the summer program because it is hot and we felt that you needed to get out for a little walk occasionally. So we developed the concept of free time. A two-block radius, north, east, south, and west. That was it."

"What about the library?"

"You can get permission to make a trip to the library. Just sign the book accordingly. Free time is for your relaxation when you don't have anything to do. But you can't just sign the book and go downtown. You have to discuss that with somebody. We always want to know your destination."

"Let me explain to you why we want you to give us a destination." Allen adjusted his glasses. "You look back on your own behavior. Nine times out of ten, when you wound up taking a shot that you didn't want to take, it was because you were wandering around idly with no purpose, no direction, no set destination in your mind. Actually it was not instituted for a program this large, it was instituted when we were in cramped quarters, to give a guy an opportunity to go out and stretch his legs instead of sitting in a cramped room. The idea was to make you think of someplace to go before you go out on free time. It's not that we are trying to play police or something. We only want to protect you from your own weak impulses. Now you can do this honestly or dishonestly. If you do it dishonestly, we still haven't helped you. If you say that you are going to Twenty-fifth Street and get a soda but you go to Twenty-seventh Street and buy a bag of dope, we haven't helped. Free time gives you a chance to walk out in the street all by yourself, to see whether or not you are strong. And, at the same time, if you find you are not strong, you come right back in the house—you get what I mean?—until you become strong.

"Rich, someone has put something on the agenda about the stoop. Should I just pass that over? No? Okay. There has been loud and boisterous noise on the stoop. We will try and assist you in developing normal behavioral patterns when you are on the stoop. We will instruct you on what kind of behavior you should exhibit while you are out there. We are not saying that you cannot stand on the stoop. But don't use the wrong kind of language with some of the civilians around here. Your intentions may be good—and sometimes they are—but be very careful how you get involved. The whole community is looking at us. We just moved here. To a degree they are a little apathetic. But at the same time, let anything happen here and the first thing they will say is those dope fiends, blah, blah, blah. Be careful how you handle yourself on the stoop. Be a gentleman at all times. Be careful even about how you go about flirting with the women. Either don't flirt or pick your people to flirt with. Don't flirt with nobody that's going to turn around and scream rape. Or smack you on the side of the jaw and you gonna pull your knife. Then we got a problem. You understand what I mean? You can do anything you want out there as long as it is under control. As long as it is decent. And acceptable by the people in the neighborhood. For example, one day one of you came up to me and took my cigarette out of my hand. This guy—I won't mention his name—just put his greasy hand out, lit his, and then wanted to give mine back to me. I didn't want to smoke out of his dirty hands. He and I hassled out there, and he had been hassling with the telephone man before that. I don't know what he had against the telephone man. The man is here to fix our phones and he's out there arguing with the telephone man. He had gone beyond acceptable behavior. I think he was tired or something—at least I hope he was tired.

"Oh: let me say this about outside jobs. We encourage you to work, but not if it interferes with your rehabilitation. You come in tired too many days and we're going to pull you off your job. There are at least two people here who have had to give up their jobs as their discipline. Or we will tell you that your passes are cancelled because you are not sleeping enough. Or, if we find you are drinking, we might decide that if you didn't have the job you couldn't get to where you could buy the lush. When you come in here, you are agreeing to place more emphasis on your personal rehabilitation than on anything else. You are, in essence, agreeing that even if you get a girl that you love and if she conflicts with your program of learning to live again, she's got to go. This is what you agree to when you come to the house—above and beyond family, friends, relatives, girlfriends, job; anything else. The first thing is you. You're the only person my interest is in. I hope you understand that."

Allen paused. He bummed a cigarette. Everybody was paying close attention. "The most important thing is you. And if you can learn to live, then you can get a thousand girls. You can get a hundred jobs when you sober up and start, you know, doing the right things. See, it all starts in here. This is what we are trying to orient you towards. Once you get that, then all these other things can be taken care of. You understand?"

A noisy mob of kids were playing outside and Allen went to the window. "Mike," he said, "you better get out there. Those kids are tearing up your scooter."

About six of them were bouncing on my Vespa, one trying to kick the starter. As gently as possible, I got them off and moved it to a gas station around the corner. I found the attendant with a pint of gin behind the grease rack. He said I could park it; one dollar please. I ran back, hoping not to have missed too much.

Mr. Randolph had the floor. "Mr. Allen, I have something I would like to be clear on, as a matter of fact it's been bothering me all night. It's about social activities. We came into a little dialogue yesterday regarding the opera."

"Oh, *everybody* has to go to the opera."

"That takes precedence over passes?"

"I want everybody to go to the opera, because I suspect that a great majority of you have never been to an opera."

"Mr. Allen, you know—I live with these fellows. Now, I will get on them if I think they are wrong. At the same time, I want them to hold on to the privileges they have, and to carry a man to the opera without any explanation of the story of the opera—he's just not going to enjoy it. If it's done in the right manner, well and good, but first things first. Now, I respect Mrs. Kosof's ability but—"

"Wait a minute, wait a minute, Mr. Randolph. Mrs. Kosof has already stated that before opera or ballet she will conduct one group session explaining what it is all about and, after they go, hold another group session for further interpretation and to get their reaction to it."

"Look, Mr. Allen," Mr. Randolph said with all due respect. "Some of these guys don't even know that William Tell shot a apple off his kid's head."

"Right. In fact, I always thought he shot the kid."

"What I'm saying is . . ." Mr. Randolph paused during heavy laughter, which he did not participate in.

"Seriously, Mr. Randolph . . . hold it fellas, this is serious." Allen waited for silence. "Seriously, I questioned her very carefully when she first proposed the idea. I said, 'How are you going to take these guys to an opera? Opera doesn't fit into our way of life.' And her point was that a whole lot of things don't fit into our way of life because we've never seen them or had an opportunity to understand or enjoy them. I'm inclined to agree with that. If it was left up to us, Randy, all we would want to do is go out on Friday and Saturday night and get a broad and lay up. I'm not talking about individuals, but as a group. You know? So what she wants to do is expose us to things we never saw before."

"I understand what you're saying, I understand. You see, that wasn't clarified to me and I didn't want anyone going to the opera and coming back here with a long face and give us a whole lot of negative response the next day."

"Sir?" Lindy raised his hand, looking dubious. "Sir, opera is pretty hard to get into. You know? First of all we ain't familiar with the music. Second, we don't understand what's happenin'; we don't understand what the singin' is about. We gonna be in trouble . . . but I guess if it's programmed. . . ."

"It's programmed. It's programmed. Let me tell you something, Lindy. She isn't scheduling an opera every week. This is once a month, once every two months maybe—whenever she can get tickets. Maybe once a year. But opera is one of those things you ought to be exposed to. There are a hundred of these things, and when you tell me 'they don' understand it, they ain't gonna like it, they gonna be uncomfortable,' why, I simply say to you that this is the same thing that a man faced when he first shot dope. And the only way he got comfortable was by constantly repeatin' the procedure."

Allen has excellent diction and can speak grammatically. Sometimes he changes, however, using dialect, articulation, and pitch like an actor. He has an orator's instinct for communication. He pushed his glasses up his nose, reverting to his Establishment role. "You are going to be exposed to a variety of things . . . just put your hands down . . . let me continue. I'll remember you—all four of you—when I'm through.

"What I'm saying is that, while some of you may not ever go to another opera, some of you may. And I want to expose these people to it. It's like this . . . you want to buy a pair of pants. You don't buy the first pair that you see, even though you may like that pair. You look at some more pants to make sure. This is what you are doing, shopping for social involvement. And in shopping for social involvement, you will be exposed to a lot of things: opera, ballet, jazz, plays, movies —you name it.

"But now let me tell you something else. You are falling into the same old trap that we always fall into when we kick a habit—and it is this. Every single thing I ever set up for guys who have kicked a habit, their first reaction was 'I don' wanna go.' Isn't that right, Mr. Ford?"

Irving Ford is an early graduate from ARC. He comes back once a week or so to see old friends and keep from slipping. Mr. Ford is a plain-looking black person; on the street you probably wouldn't look twice at him. His clothes are poor but neat, his face neither coarse nor particularly interesting. He has, however, one of the gentlest smiles I've ever seen. Mr. Ford smiled.

"Remember when you were still in the house? They were having jazz concerts up at the library, and plays and poetry readings. The first time we set something up . . . you want to tell it baby?"

"We almost had a fight," Mr. Ford said. "B.B. here, boy, he was so mad goin' up there . . . whew. 'I don' wanna go to no poetry readin',' he kept sayin'. We had to drag him up there, but after we left, why he's sayin', 'When can I go back?' A lotta other guys didn't wanna go either, because they felt they wouldn't like poetry readin'. But one thing bothers me . . . can I say somethin'?"

"Sure, go ahead, Mr. Ford."

"Well, this opera thing is groovy, you know what I mean, but I don't think it should be embedded in a person's mind that he's not cultivated unless he likes the opera."

"Who says you're not cultivated?"

"To me it adds up somethin' like, you nothin' unless you like opera. It's a snob thing."

"We seem to have a lot of guys in the house that don't like opera, or at least I am getting that opinion. How many of you guys have ever seen an opera?"

"I have."

"Where?"

"In Oklahoma."

"Me too."

"Where?"

"At the Ernie Pyle Theatre in Tokyo."

"Where did you see yours?"

"Metropolitan Opera."

"Which one did you see?"

"Madame Butterfly."

"All right. We have three people here who have seen an opera and ten who haven't. Now what is wrong with exposing these ten to an opera? Some of you might really dig an opera. There is no reason in the world why, if somebody interprets what's going to happen and you have a program in front of you explaining the action, you can't understand it. I think that what you're doing is evaluating these men as being less intelligent than they are. They can dig anything. You're talking about a group of guys who have been digging all their lives. I bet they come back and half of them enjoy it."

Garwood Cole wears an embroidered cap. He is also known

as "Garwood X." His handsome blue-black face was scowling, his eyes gleaming intensely. "I don't think I'll dig opera," he says, "and I'm not—"

"I'm not sayin' you'll dig it, just . . ." Allen was losing patience.

"I'm askin' to be excused."

"I doubt that I'm gonna grant that, Garwood, because as far as I can see, you never participate in social activities."

"I do participate. I explained to Mrs. Kosof that I have my own social activity pertainin' to my religion."

"Does your religion state that you can't go to the opera?"

"It states not to any European operas."

"Then you are going to have to show me this in your rules."

"I'll bring it to you tomorrow."

"All right, you do that, Mr. C. All right, that settles the opera. . . ."

"No, no, no." Hands went up. Lindy Stokes was recognized. "Mr. Allen, all them operas are in Eyetalian or some language like that. How we goin' to understand anythin' even if the story is explained to us beforehand?"

Allen worked hard at keeping his cool, repeating with resignation, "I suspect that you are going to have enough interpretation to understand what is going on. I suspect that. Look, you didn't understand dope shootin' either, but you enjoyed it . . . you don't dig what John Coltrane is playin', but you like that . . . you don't understand what Miriam Makeba is singin' but you—"

"Ethnic preferences have something to do with that," Mr. Randolph said.

"Hold it, hold it." Everyone is talking at once. "Lemme tell you somethin' about this group. And it is simply this. Here we are, a bunch of guys who want to meet and get involved in society. Some of you say to me, 'Man, how can I get a little girl?' But you won't go any place where the girls go. Sometimes some of you go up to 126th Street—well, that's the worst crowd. Ain't nothin' up there but whoos . . . right? So why don't you expose yourself to an atmosphere where decent women go? Who knows, you might pull one of them little opera girls. You may laugh at this, see, but I'm pointin' out to you that nothing is impossible. It's just as easy to go out there and get a broad at the opera as anywhere else.

"Or, you may go down to smoke at intermission and meet some responsible citizen. You speak and you get to know each other. It might work into a very profitable relationship. One thing is for certain and that is this: if you need and want money to better your condition, you gonna have to get around people who are bettering their condition, or who have money. If you need a hundred dollars, you'd probably get it quicker by being around people who got money than you would around people who ain't got no money. Right? So all I'm doing is exposing you to some of what is considered to be the better elements of society so that perhaps some of it will rub off. You got on a white suit and you want to keep it white, you don't get out there and start rollin' around in the street. The street is dirty. What you should do is make sure that you walk in places where that suit will stay white.

"All of you is always cryin' to me, 'I ain't got nothin' to do. . . .' " Allen mimicked a whine, looking at the faces around him. The room was silent except for the fish tank pump chugging away. "So all I'm doin' is givin' you something to do besides sit around here; simply somethin' to do.

"Wouldn't you rather be sittin' in the opera than sittin' in the park shootin' dope? All I'm doin' is giving you some activity that don't involve shootin' dope, things that other people do. And you say to me, 'Why don't you give me something besides the opera?' I'm giving you the opera *and* something else too. I'm giving *all* of it to you. You can choose what you want to get involved with. This is all. It's that simple.

"Look." Allen stood up and started pacing. "It's costing ninety-six dollars an hour to run this place. And I'm not spending ninety-six dollars an hour unless I make sure that it is spent for things that can benefit you. The opera is one of these things."

"Is that how you feel about it?" Garwood asked. "Or is that how Mrs. Kosof feels about it? I think that black man's history is more important. I think that's just as beneficial to our education as the opera."

"This is scheduled for you too; black man's history is mandatory too. But understand this: this is my belief, anyway. As long as we live in this country called America, we ought to expose ourselves to all of the different aspects of the so-called American way of life. Because as long as we live here, somehow we gotta come in contact with these people, and we ought to know something about their behavior. And we ought to know not from what we read, but from what we can experience. Then, perhaps, we can compare it with what we read and make our own personal evaluation. This is why *all* these things are mandatory."

"Could you explain just what Mrs. Kosof's duties are?"

"All right, let me explain to you in general what her job is. When you come here you say, in essence, 'I need help so that I can begin to live normally.' Her job is to assist you in achieving a level of normal living in your social and recreational involvement, just like you achieve in other aspects of the program. Let me cite to you what I mean. As far as abstaining from using drugs, you're living normally. As far as work is concerned—vocationally—you're living normally. There is one area that you would admit that you have not come up to a normal level in, and that's your social area. Her job is to assist you in reaching that level in your social life."

"I thought she was a psychiatrist. She wanted to know what was bugging me; was it something in my childhood."

"Let me tell you this about my own personal rehabilitation—I can only go by my own experiences. My own personal rehabilitation was strengthened by me relating to all kinds of people. What I'm saying is that sometimes you think you can get more from talking to some broad who doesn't know nothing about psychiatry, than if you talk to an accredited psychiatrist. This is something that you'll have to decide. I'm not saying that you are right or wrong, you know, 'cause I don't know. I don't know how much strength you could have gotten or how much development could have been effected by you telling her these things that she was asking. It may have helped and it may not. It may very well be that maybe your social life is dragging because of something that happened in your childhood. I don't know. I do know in my own life that—and I cite this to you for a fact—that socially I had a hang-up as far as broads was concerned.

"When I was a kid, I remember a thousand times over my father sneaking out of somebody's room that he didn't have any business in—and you know what this did to me? It created an impression that my father was a mad lover—you know, any woman he wanted he could get. And I sort of grew up with this same thing, you know, walking in dad's footsteps. For a long time this was my hang-up. I didn't know how to talk to a woman socially, unless I was tryin' to make her. So you see sometimes our childhood has a bearing on our social involvement."

Somebody whose name I don't know, who left the Center a week later, says, "That's what Whitey have done to our black women. He made 'em all whores."

"You're sayin' you don't like Whitey. This is your prerogative. This is something that you yourself will have to decide. I can tell you quite honestly there are some white people I trust, and there are some I don't. And there are some black people I trust and there are some I don't.

"And lemme tell you somethin'. If you restricted yourself to jazz as the only form of, say, positive behavior you participate in, it would not necessarily be because you like the music or because of any ethnic considerations but because of the connotations and the character of a lot of people that you've met around jazz, related to dope. What I'm sayin' to you is this: you will negate anything that's not either directly or indirectly related to gettin' high. And this is why, time and again, we force you into situations. For example, when I first said to the house group that you can't stay out after twelve o'clock, this also was considered negatively. When I first said you got to save money, you griped at that. In fact, I can't think of a single thing in this program that people have not griped at.

"So all I am saying to you now is that it's high time that you started to dig yourself and realize that all that negative thinking has gotten your mind so disorganized that you really are *not* in a position to plan your own involvement. And that you ought to be glad of two things. That first of all, that the planning is being done by somebody who knows what you were involved in and who has a decent idea of the things that you ought to be exposed to. And I'm not talkin' about Kosof now, I'm talkin' about me.

"All I'm tryin' to do is to keep B.B. from goin' out in the streets and spendin' fifty dollars a day for ten days and windin' up right back in the same old rut that he was in when he first came here, to keep him from taking six months of sober living and throwing it down the drain in ten days. I'm tryin' to set up a program where when a man gets off drugs and stays off two years he develops to a point that he won't just go out on the street and blow that two years like blowin' money in a crap game. I'm tryin' to fix it so that you can feel free to go out there in the street and live and move anywhere you want to live and move, without becoming ensnared in the perils of drugs again. And I'm doing this because I want to see you live decent and because you say you want to. I'm not going through this frustration to play a game with you. Look, I'm losin' my hair in the process and the only reason I lose my hair is because I think—I really believe—that you people are just as decent and respectable as anybody else, because I'm you, I'm *one* of you. And *I* like to be considered decent and respectable. But I can't do it unless you help me. Is that clear? Okay!"

Chairs scraped. People stretched, gathering in small groups. Others put on their coats and split right away.

Allen came over to my corner, scratching and nodding like a pro. "Hey, baby," he said, acting out the junkie rasp and posture. "Hey, baby, howdja dig the scene? Sheeeit . . . pretty groovy. Somethin' else. Right?" He stuck out his hand for some skin and scratched a cheek with the other as he sank himself to the floor . . . finally breaking out of it with a gusty laugh. "Really," he asked, "how did you enjoy the session?"

"Very interesting," I said. "There's only one thing though—I hate opera. Can I be excused?"

Allen leaned back to laugh; a hearty, contagious laugh—the laugh of a free man.

The kids were no longer playing around the automobile wrecks. As usual, the white cops, in and out of uniform, walked to and from the precinct house, which gives 123rd Street a deceptive peace—the eye of a hurricane.

The fall sun was sinking. It was still warm and I looked forward to the scooter ride downtown through Central Park. Kicking the starter, I noticed the gas station attendant was completely out of it, his head on the desk in the funky office. The jug of gin was next to him—empty.

From *New Life* (ARC newsletter):

THE VOICE

For three years I have not used drugs because I was in prison, also, I am a Muslim. The reason I stated that I am a Muslim is because I am being condemned and indirectly being attacked for what I am by those who profess to be good Christians. Let's settle this now, I respect a man for what he is but my respect is being taken as a weakness by those who profess to be Christians within the Addicts Rehabilitation Center and outside I came for help not for a religious argument. This act of being indirectly attacked is an act of stupidity and lack of understanding. There is a philosophy that they use at the center. They say they do not force a person to stop using drugs. This should apply to religion also. If he or she wants to stop using drugs, let him make that choice the same as becoming a Christian or a Muslim or Hindu or Jew.

When you try to force something on somebody they rebel against it, am I wrong for what I am saying? No! For in Islam we Muslims say

> "Glory to Allah the most high, full of grace and mercy. He created all, He created man, He gave man a special place in his creation. He honored man to be his Agent until that end, endued with understanding, purified his affection so that he

> should have spiritual insight, understand nature, understand himself and glorify Allah in truth, reference and unity. For the forfillment of this great trust, man was further given a will so that his acts should reflect Allah's universal will and law and his mind should experience the sublime joy of being in harmony with the infinite and the great drama of the world around him and his own spiritual growth."

But created through He was in the best of Moulds, Man fell from unity, he chose the crooked path of discord, sorrow and pain, selfishness, arrogance and hatred. He saw the shapes of evil in the physical, moral and spiritual world and in himself. When men spread themselves over the earth speaking diverse language, learning diverse customs and laws; the evils became multiplied first between individual and secondly between nations.

Man began to fear the strong and oppress the weak and to curse in adversity and to pursue phantoms. For the truth and reality was gone from their minds, but Allah forgives and guides individuals and nations and turn to good what to us seems evil. So I say let he or she chose what they want to be or believe. Let us settle our drug problems and set a goal to the road of respect. We must not let negative thoughts divert us from the road of success of being respected beings.

Garwood Cole

8
On a Downhill Drag

Group therapy at ARC is not scientific. More an enforced rap, it can sometimes be merely a two-hour speech by the leader of the day. Often, however, the chemistry works and they get down to some kind of nitty. The subject matter is not limited to dope. Anything that will make the man think, re-evaluate his life, is considered pertinent.

This session, under the direction of Anna Kosof, was starting hard. Anna is twenty-three, born in Hungary. She seems older. The way she smiles, sadly, with only half of her round, pale face, indicates an understanding beyond her years of how hopelessly fucked up everything is. But she must try anyway. Being white and straight, however, Anna is by definition a complete square. That distance will always remain; goodwill can never completely overcome it. It was particularly noticeable as she tried to get her session off the ground one Thursday afternoon.

There was no response to the first of four ethnic records she had selected to base the session on: Leon Bibb singing a slave song. "Look over yonder . . . Coo-Coo Bird . . . I pray Lord . . . Lordy Lordy . . ." That kind of thing.

Absolute silence. Anna waited in front of the blackboard, playing with two pieces of chalk. Nothing. "You are shaking your heads," she said. "Would you like me to play it again?"

A low, reluctant chorus said yes. Once more.

"What do you think he's singing about?" More silence. Some cigarettes were lit. "Rocky, what do you think?"

"I pass," Rocky said, looking down.

"Wash?"

"What do I think it's about? I would think it's an effort . . . it sounds like the man has been workin' and he's been beaten down . . ." Wash struggles with words.

"Well, what condition was he in?"

". . . I didn't notice."

Nobody seemed to feel any identification with Leon Bibb's version of slavery. Henry finally volunteered, ". . . Like my man Wash here says: he's singin' about it's a long way, a never-endin' day. You know, sun been turnin' over and he's in misery, almost dead. You know, that Old Man River bit. . . ."

B.B. tried to be helpful by suggesting she play it back at a slower speed so maybe "the words come in more clear."

"I don't think it will make any difference . . . well, maybe we should go on to something else. The first song goes back a hundred years. This next one though is fairly contemporary." Anna speaks with a slight, consonant, East European accent.

Oscar Brown, Jr. sang. ". . . I want you to stand up tall and proud . . . to speak clear and loud . . . Brown Baby. . . ."

"Would you like to hear it again?" . . . Silence . . . "I don't hear any answer. . . ."

"No, no. I thought it was extremely clear." This is a hard-looking chick with badly scarred arms and nappy hair bleached bright blonde. Her face looks like it hasn't smiled in years.

"If it is so clear, what is he really saying?" Mrs. Kosof asked.

"He's promising his child a better world—that's what I hear. What I get is a parent speaking to his child, telling him to stand tall, be proud of his color, to be a man. . . ."

A bunch of dogs began howling and barking in the alley.

Harlem dogs are different; beasts, not pets. Outlaws. One imagines them eating garbage, fighting with big rats and each other. Their wild sound reflects the territory they live in.

Wash has just been appointed a staff apprentice and he smiles a lot; even the top of his shaved head goes along. "Well, er, uh, he's talkin' about freedom. In the first song the man had little hope . . . but in the second he had more hope . . . I mean, he spoke of freedom for the next generation. In the first song he had no hope for any . . . very sad. . . ."

"Rocky, what do you think?"

"I don't have anything to say at this time."

"Do you really mean to say that this doesn't affect you at all?"

"I have nothing to say . . . the whole meeting affects me. Well, I'm here to learn something, but it's a subject I don't particularly care for and I prefer not to say anything."

Rocky came down to my place twice. Just having had it painted, I asked Rich Feimster if any of the guys were available to help me straighten it out. He picked Rocky, suggested I pay $1.25 an hour, and would I call him right after Rocky left at the end of the day.

As we moved furniture, swept up, and washed windows together, I often caught him staring at me. He asked how much money I made, what I did last summer, do I have a girl, what it's like to be a writer. "Mike, I can't figure you out," he said. "You know, I wonder what's on your mind when you're up there with us."

Rocky has a habit of sucking in air as he searches for words. A stocky man in his forties, he is a veteran of the big war, spent some time in the south of France and has been to California. We discussed those places.

When I asked if he wanted some coffee, he answered

quickly: "Sure—and how about a little—you know . . . it's cold outside." He licked his lips in anticipation.

"Are you sure it's all right?" I felt so goddam square.

"Oh, come on. Not you too."

I poured some brandy into his cup, knowing it was against the rules. "You're not supposed to do this, are you?"

"Man, I'm havin' a tough time," he admitted. "It's weird, what makes a man stay in there? It's not like a jail or anything, you know. There's nothin' keepin' us from walkin' out the door. It's hard, it's a hard thing to do. I wonder, you know, why am I here? I was never really down and out, like in the gutter. I always kept myself clean, took my One-A-Day vitamins every morning, had myself a pad on Riverside Drive and 146th Street. My girl used to come over and do little things for it, like girls do.

"Every afternoon I'd go out and get what I needed for tomorrow. I'd need about sixty, seventy-five dollars a day. Some days I'd only get twenty-five, thirty maybe, but the next day it might be three, four hundred and I'd get myself half a load and then I'd have some time to spend with my girl—wouldn't have to push so hard. I always had access to people with narcotics. Maybe that's what was wrong. I was never really greasy out there.

"And I never could stand rules—always kind of gone my own way. I know it sounds funny, but I don't feel too much in common with the other guys in the program. All they ever do is talk about dope and broads. And I don't like livin' in Harlem—never have. It's too confinin'."

"But isn't it worth investing a year to save the rest of your life?" I asked him. "It's really nothing compared to the prospect of growing old and being too weak to hustle every day. Then what do you do? And probably you won't even grow old if you keep it up, or if you do it will be in jail."

"Yeah, you got a point there. I know that. But with you

it's different. It's easy for you to talk. Like, in six months you'll probably be in the south of France or some place like that, thinkin' about the house—but I'll still be in it. It's a very hard thing, Mike. If only I could beat this thing. . . ."

Rocky is from Baltimore. After his army discharge he worked for some people who owned a small chain of cleaning stores there. They taught him the business and the advisability of being frugal. He saved his bread and left with their blessing to open his own store. After a thorough survey of some neighborhoods, he picked the right block. He gave good service, built a clientele and prospered for a few years. The officers at the bank knew him and called him by his last name. He had a line of credit.

Since the store wasn't far from the port, many of his customers were sailors. Which was his undoing. For sailors, as is well known, tend to be wild in port. One day this particular gob picking up three suits pulled out an envelope of white powder and sniffed some in front of Rocky, who didn't know what the hell it was.

Then the same old story; a hidden need fulfilled. It made him sick but he tried it again the next time the sailor came in. And the next. He soon began buying a supply to tide him over. It was cheap, it made him feel good, he had plenty of money anyway and he didn't know it built.

His business wasn't hurt—he lost it. The store, his savings—everything. He eventually moved to New York, just like everybody else, where the dope is better, cheaper, and easier to cop. Now he sits around the center wondering why he's there.

Rocky stared out my bedroom window. It is a view I do my best to avoid: the Apex Technical School across the street. That cross section of functional classrooms with men of all ages and colors trying to get ahead on their own time reminds me of crowded subways, or anonymous projects of people piled with carefully chosen furniture on top of each other, or clean cars packed with dirty, impatient kids on Sunday expressways—the teeming masses in general. Start thinking of that in New York and you can get pretty depressed.

Rocky has a different view. "That's nice over there," he said. "People trying to improve themselves . . . nice." He stood there looking for a while.

Leaving, Rocky told me what a good time he'd had, how groovy it was to talk to somebody who had traveled and knew something of the world. Next time I needed help, I must call him—he was my man. He made me promise.

I said I was looking for someone to clean up once a week but he probably wouldn't want that sort of thing. He was very excited though. "Sure. Great. Don't forget now, it's a promise." He would keep me in top-notch shape.

His second time will be the last. From the beginning it was all wrong. He asked for the café royal right away and poured himself another. His first chore was sweeping the stairs. After making a surly stab at it for about ten minutes, he came back and said, "Mike, I didn't know this was what you had in mind. That's women's work. I think you oughta get a woman to do it."

"But I told you. . . ." I stopped myself, realizing the futility of reason under these circumstances. I would have liked to tell him about Zev Putterman sweeping up in Synanon, to point out what he was doing to himself. But he was far from open. Rocky has a long way to go.

"I'll get somebody else—don't worry about it," I said.

The staff is worried about Rocky. They discuss him often. The pull back is still too strong. They would not be surprised to lose him. He stays by himself, watching television or just staring. He never reads. At therapy sessions he has nothing to say. Anna didn't press him. "Okay," she said. "Let's play the next record."

My skin is black, my arms are long
My hair is wooly, my back is strong
Strong enough to take the pain
Inflicted again and again,
What do they call me? My name is "Aunt Sarah"

My skin is yellow, my hair is long
Between two worlds I do belong
My father was rich and white
He forced my mother late one night
What do they call me? My name is "Safronia"

My skin is tan, my hair is fine
My hips invite you, my mouth like wine
Who's little girl am I?
Anyone who has money to buy
What do they call me? My name is "Sweet Thing"

My skin is brown, my manner is tough
I'll kill the first mother I see
My life has been rough
I'm awfully bitter these days because my parents
were slaves,
What do they call me? My name is "Peaches" *

"What do these four women symbolize? . . . Norman?"

Norman speaks with a deep baritone. His glasses are taped together. "I think it symbolizes the Negro race as a whole . . . we don't know who our fathers are . . . that's what I think it is; an awareness of the Negro race."

"Rocky?"

"I don't have any comment."

* "Four Women," words and music by Nina Simone (ASCAP).

Norman had his hand up again. "Mrs. Kosof, you're asking for opinions. I don't see how you could possibly understand. You have to look at it from the point of view of a white person. No matter how much you associated with us, or knew us or any Negro, you couldn't get from that record what we could. . . ."

"I think that song was written for white people." Henry has a moustache and always wears a hat. "We're familiar with all of that. It needs no describing for us. We've been living it for a hundred years. . . ."

"That's right," Norman interrupted. "Like Mr. Henry says, we've been living it and no matter how hard you try you couldn't get the feeling we would. You ask, 'What do you get out of this?' You will get one thing, we will get another. I don't think there is any meeting of the minds as far as this is concerned. This is my opinion."

The pace picked up. Anna had trouble keeping things orderly. The early lethargy was over. Is hate replacing fear of Whitey? Can any white person understand the Negro's problems? What is the best way to get Black Power?

Anna played another record; Yaphet Kotto singing "Have you ever seen the blues? . . . Yes, I've seen the blues in your eyes . . . I listened while you told the world you was so hip . . . Man, you better call the landlord on the phone . . . All the time there wasn't a dime for food . . . no money for rent . . . I know where you at . . . You might as well be dead . . . Lord God Jesus save me . . . I know you, I know your story too . . . Have you ever seen the blues?"

"Yeah," Henry said without being asked. "Look, you tie a man up and you leave him there a long time. He's real hungry. Then you come along and wave some food in his face and you release him. Through the years this man been seeing Whitey in his big cars so as soon as he gets the chance, instead of taking first things first, he goes out and imitates him. You know, big cars, pretty clothes and all . . . and he can't even afford the rent or food. He had to set his pattern after the white man. He had no other pattern to set than the white man's. So he goes out and buys him a Cadillac and a lotta suits, you know, and it makes a big man out of him. That's what it's about."

Mrs. Boatright opened the door. She is the bookkeeper. Young, tall, a bit heavy, with close-cropped hair, she has beautiful eyes which have never been clouded with junk. Flashing a smile at Mrs. Kosof, she sat in a corner and listened.

The discussion continued. Is suffering universal? I don't feel hate for Whitey, don't misunderstand me, it's not hate that I feel. People got to do somethin' for themselves 'stead of cryin' 'bout it; you've got to step forward. There could never be a real tough relationship between a slave and a slave master. We still are slave and slave master in an indirect sense; like, they out there, they. Whitey in general.

"So," Mrs. Kosof said. "Is there no hope for us to understand each other? Do you feel, for example, that an addict can never understand a square and vice versa?"

Rocky shook his head and muttered, "Sheeeit," while Wash wrinkled his crown, waving a hand for the floor.

"I think there's no parallel because all addicts and ex-addicts have been square at one time or another. I can't explain it exactly, but I don't think a white man could ever understand a black man's suffering, no matter how much suffering of his own he did. It's not the same, a suffering where there's a lack of hope. . . . When Whitey gets out of whatever bind he's in, he's free. But with a Negro, he could get out and he's still not out. . . ."

"May I say something?" Mrs. Boatright is articulate. She is writing a play. "Our problem is unique. You know, I'd like to put this into historical context. Do you realize the bloody riots there were when the Irish tried to gain their freedom? And what about the trouble the Jews had when they first came here? Our problem is not unique. There's one big difference though. The Irish could assimilate because they are the same color. Even Jewish people can change their names and sneak in. But a black person—regardless of what your social strata is, your color identifies you. There are some white people who understand this, but those few who do understand don't make the policy of this country. They are in the minority like we are; they are just as isolated as we are. But even with them, even though they have their commitment, the moral issue and all that—they are different from us because we *live* it."

"I think I'm a little more broadminded on this subject than the average Negro." Henry was slumped in his chair. He gestures when he talks. "I can understand the white man's position. He's got the world by the tail on a downhill drag. Right? And he don't wanna let go. He don't wanna share the tail with us, and I can understand it because if I had the world by the tail on a downhill drag I wouldn't wanna share it either."

You wouldn't believe the noise, the confusion . . . "Oh, man, what you sayin'? You don' know what you talkin' about."

"This is the way it is . . . it is!" Henry kept insisting. "I'm sayin' how it is! He'd be a sucker if he did let go. If I had it, as a Negro, if I had the world by the tail on a downhill drag, you think I'd share it with him? I'd be a sucker, wouldn't I? This is the situation. Well, all right. Why should we kid ourselves? This is what creates the turmoil. This is why we're demonstratin', integratin', and tryin' to get equal rights. And this is why he's fightin' not to give us equal rights. Now how many of you don't understand that?

"We're gonna have to take the power and we will eventually because there are more nonwhites than whites in the world. It may take two hundred years, but we'll have it."

"Do you mind if I don't agree with you?" Mrs. Boatright said. "It's not going to happen in this country. I just don't see it."

"It's got to be a gradual thing. You got to first get a grip on the handle, you know, before you can swing a pick."

"Before we swing any pick, we'll all be in concentration camps. The black man will never get anything near total power in this country."

"Look," the bleached chick said, "the only way we gonna get Whitey to give anything up is to start poppin' him off like they doin' to us. Next time George Wallace come to New York, somebody oughta pop him off."

"Oh, come on. They'd come up here and exterminate all of Harlem, just waste every one of us. You can't think the same way they do because you ain't got what they got. The whole black race—as far as the United States is concerned—would be wiped out."

"Mrs. Kosof?" Rocky raised his hand.

"Yes, Rocky."

"May I be excused? I don't feel well."

From *New Life* (ARC newsletter):

An "ex" anything is looked upon by some people with a small degree of nostalgia, sympathy, empathy or maybe thoughts of a has-been run through their minds. The feats of battles won, heights reached by a number of ex-gamblers etc., are all considered by the masses as non-existent professions or routines now but is this same consideration and feelings extended to an ex-addict? Do they feel that his addiction to drugs is no longer apart of his daily routine, as with the "ex's" of other routines? How long does it take to be in that category? How many times must you refuse to use drugs before you can be classed as an "ex"?

In reality, the moment you drink your last drink, fight your last fight or shoot your last shot then and right then, I believe: X MARKS THE SPOT!

FROM THE EDITOR'S DESK

For more than 100 years, the Black Man here in America has striven to achieve dignity and respect, with a carefully chosen few succeeding. The ones that have not succeeded are still imprisoned within the ghettos, receive inferior educations, economic deprivation, political disfranchisement, with fear and frustration continuously plaguing Black Citizens. Therefore, this is no time to become or be addicted to narcotics.

9
Strokes and Blokes

Flagg got busted drinking bourbon in the kitchen and was put on restriction, which is going to screw up his plans. Feeling mistreated, he asked Allen for an audience. It is in progress.

"I was put on thirty-day restriction and I don't understand—"

"For what? I haven't heard anything about it."

"For drinking."

"For drinking? And you only got thirty days? You were very lucky . . . very lucky. You should have got put out. You mean to say that you drank in here? Mr. Randolph, how come you didn't pack his bag?"

Mr. Randolph, Rich Feimster, and four of the guys have been called in to testify.

"I wasn't aware of the incident until the next morning, Mr. Allen."

"You were very lucky, Mr. Flagg, because everybody knows the rule about no drinking and . . . now, I'm going away next Sunday, the Good Lord willing, and I'll tell you something. I'll say it right in front of Rich. You are lucky it didn't happen during that time, because usually when I leave town, Mr. Feimster cleans house. So I just know that"—Allen affects a Tom drawl—"some a'yall jess ain't gonna be heah when ah gets back."

"Oh, Mr. Feimster's heart is like butter," Lindy says with a sly smile. "All you gotta do with him is not let it get too hot. I'll bet you twenty dollars that everybody's gonna be here when you get back. How long you gonna be gone?"

"Eighteen days. Let me say this. If you are here when I get back, it will be worth much more to me than twenty dollars. Much more. Let me warn you again, Mr. Flagg. You were very lucky."

"May I say something? I realize I made a little mistake. I admit that and I'm sorry for it. But a pint of bourbon don't seem to me to be worth no thirty days."

"You have to make up your own mind, man. . . ." Lately Garwood is always carrying books, memorizing things from a small tape recorder and he is in the market for a Nikon which he wants to shoot around Harlem next summer. Garwood is on staff and a member of the "Two Percenters," an inner circle. Named after the rate of cured addicts previously enjoyed by the likes of Lexington, the Two Percenters try harder than necessary by imposing their own—stricter—rules on top of the regular program. Garwood's determination is intense. ". . . It's up to you.

"This is comin' from me—myself—about drug addiction. I did a helluva turn-around in prison. I made up my own mind, back then I decided. I'm not anticipatin' the same dirty life I led before. I'm not gonna be the same no good bum. No, I'm not gonna do it. I'm gonna advance myself. The world is outside of you, man. This is why we are given a will; to choose right from wrong."

Flagg thinks Garwood is some kind of teacher's pet. "Look," he says. "I have my first gig in months, New Years' Eve. All I want is to be able to get out that one night. I'll even go along with the rest of it but I think that playing my horn is a very important part of my rehabilitation."

"Why should the rules be changed to fit you, man?" Garwood's eyes are narrowed and blazing. "Okay, you wanna go out, party . . . so on . . . drink up wine. I'm not sayin' you gonna do it, but even for a gig the rules and regulations say 'no drinking.' No hard beverages, period. I don't know, man, everybody say, 'Yeah, these rules and regulations are boss,' but then they get mad at somethin' they already agreed to. Yeah, you're good and angry, but I don't care. You can put all your blame on me. That ain't gonna do nothin' but make me more stronger. That's all it's gonna do for me. 'Cause I'm goin' to tell you somethin'. This place get to me sometimes. I've felt like I wanna quit my job. But you know what I said? I said, if I quit, this is a weakness within me so I'm gonna stay and fight it. And I'm still here. I'm functionin'. I'm goin' by the rules and regulations of the program. If you violate those rules and regulations you should suffer for it. You know I'm right but you ain't man enough to face up to it."

"Hey, Rich. How come everybody knows that Mr. Flagg got thirty days' restriction for drinking but me?"

"I didn't know we had decided that yet, Mr. Allen."

"Oh? Where did you hear that, Mr. Flagg?"

"One of the guys told me."

"One of the guys? Did he? Well, whoever it was just got you thirty days' restriction. Why don't you ask him how much of a fine we should put on you?"

A fine is a compulsory deposit in your compulsory savings account. "I think a forty-dollar fine would be just nice," Lindy says gently, smiling as usual. "I had to pay forty dollars last week myself, and I think it would be only fair to put forty dollars into the bank for his very own self. Mr. Flagg, you know, I've gonc out of the guidelines sometimes and I've been popped for it. Well, when I get popped for doin' somethin' that I know is my fault I'm not goin' to offer any defense. I'm just gonna say I'm sorry. 'Cause I know what the rules are and I know when I'm wrong.

"I had something very important to do last weekend. But when I went for that pass and Mr. Randolph said, 'Don't be ridiculous, son, you know you can't cop no pass. You be lucky if you get out by Easter,' I understood this, man. Sure

I was disturbed about it, but not because they kept me in the house—because I goofed. It was my goof that kept me in the house last weekend. I've got nobody to blame but myself."

"But Mr. Allen, I've been here seven months now. At what point are we supposed to start making our own decisions? Don't you feel that some people have stronger personalities than others? Take your case for example. . . ."

"I set myself up a program. There was no program so I established my own. Some people are strong enough to do this, others aren't. My personal opinion is that you are not ready to make your own decisions yet. Remember what happened with Mr. Press . . . ?"

There had been a bad scene with Press. It was just after the program moved to its present quarters from the loft around the corner. A $250,000 grant from the New York State Narcotics Addiction Control Commission had been approved but was still not received. Everybody was up-tight. There was no money so few activities could be planned and the guys were at loose ends, especially on weekends. Practically the entire house was on some kind of restriction. One Sunday morning Press was caught smoking pot in his room.

The shame of it is that Press had been in the program for over a year and, although he didn't know it, was about to become staff. Instead, he was put on probation and indefinite restriction, both of which he accepted stoically. His only beef was with the fink.

All of this was hanging out during a Saturday session, when the program received three visitors from downtown: Dr. Mitchell Rosenthal, Frank Natale, and Candy Latson, all with the City Rehabilitation program under Dr. Efram Ramirez. Rosenthal is second in command.

Addict rehabilitation centers are competitors; they exchange operating information about as freely as United States Steel and Bethlehem. Some are publicly funded, some not. Most use ex-addicts in executive positions now, paying them as much as $13,000 a year to start. A clean addict is becoming a valuable commodity.

Being independent and small, Allen is vulnerable and should be polite to the Establishment whether or not he wants to. He had reluctantly invited Rosenthal, but not the other two. All three auditing the session would destroy it so he took them up to his office. They were there almost an hour.

Afterwards, Allen was good and angry. Pacing as he talked, he pushed his glasses up his nose more often than usual. "Do you know this guy got mad as hell at me because I wouldn't let him and his cronies come into the meeting. I used as my reason the fact that they were strangers and we were going to talk about some things that were going to make you people mad . . . and this is true.

"Mr. Press was smoking pot upstairs. First of all, do you know what would happen to the program if the police knew that? And imagine if Rosenthal and his cronies had come in while we were dealing with this kind of problem. Mr. Press should know better by now.

"To me, the most important thing is what is best for you. I'm not trying to impress them. I'd like to explain that this man is directly from OCAP, Office of the Coordinator. He came up here to evaluate this program in terms of giving us money. Now, I might have treated him in such a way that they may decide that they don't want to help us. Rosenthal may go back and report that this is a lousy program . . . they may decide that they're not going to give us any money. . . .

"But I didn't want to expose you—even though you're jiving. We may not even have a program after today because he is the person who decides whether or not our program is fit to keep going. I wouldn't mind that as much as if somebody here pretending to program destroyed the program. What would hurt me no end is if I worked nine long years to try and build a program and some idiot in here, thinking he was loyal according to the code of the street, would not come up and tell me that some other idiot is doing something that could destroy the program. I mean that.

"I understand Mr. Press has said he didn't realize he was livin' with a bunch of informers. When you come in that door, you ought to make up your mind that all of the crap you had going out in the street—you know, this loyalty, 'ratting' business and so forth—that you gonna leave that outside the door. . . . Yeah, Garwood. You had your hand up."

"I just wanted to say . . . you know more about my case than anybody else. When I first came into this program . . . I actually didn't wanna come to be truthful. But I didn't have a house to go to. My family had doubts that I would ever be anything, or try to do anything for myself. So, if not for this program I would have—if necessary to keep from starving to death out in that street—I would have returned to stickin' up stores, knockin' somebody on the head and all those other things to get what I wanted.

"But once I came in here I seen that the program offered me a lot. And I programmed because this is what I was lookin' for—somethin' to do for myself. Sometimes I be wonderin' if the guys in the program realize what happens if this guy . . . what's his name? . . . Rosenthal . . . what happens if he gets an unfavorable impression. I be thinkin', 'Do they actually care about the program?'

"Then, when they get caught they get a beef. 'Oh, man, what?!!! You the pohleece or somethin'?' Yeah, I'm goin' to be the pohleece, you better believe it. I'm not gonna let nobody put me in the street, boy. 'Cause I ain't got nothin' but a little chump-change. And how long's that chump-change gonna feed me in the street. Y'all can sit up here and say, 'Man, he don't know what he's talkin' about,' but the hawk's around the corner and I'm not gonna freeze for nobody."

". . . Well, Press wasn't ready yet. That was our mistake. We're not going to make it again. Mr. Flagg, you went out the prescribed guidelines, guidelines that you people set up, not us.

"Some of you in here have your own idea of how you want to be rehabilitated. You are like hitchhikers, and the program is your ride. Any place the program turns in a direction you think is different from the way you are going, you want to get off. And ninety percent of the people who get off will go right out in the street and fall flat on their face . . . then come back and ask for another ride.

"What you don't understand is that your own reasoning and planning is what got you where you was when you came in the program in the first place and that the only way you gonna get out of going back there is by giving up all your reasoning and planning. Don't you see? This is where your dope habit came from—your own reasoning and planning—let me hear some feedback."

"Mr. Flagg, I don't think you know when you are well off," Lindy says. "I tried that program downtown . . . where that guy Rosenthal came from. I went in there and they ask me, 'How long you got that moustache?' I say, 'Ten years.' They say, 'Well, shave it off.' I says to myself, well it's not that big a thing, I'll shave it off. Then they say, 'Take off all that hair.' And I say, 'Okay, I'll take a haircut—not that big a deal.' The next morning I'm goin' down to the john and a guy says, 'Where you goin'?' I say, 'I'm goin' to the toilet.' The man say, 'Somebody got to go in there and watch you flush.' 'Man, watch me flush? Where you think I'm from?

What do you think I am?' The man say, 'You ain't nothin', you shit.'

"Now, I don't believe in all that destructive stuff. Soul brothers got enough of that as it is. I came back up here and *begged* Mr. Allen to take me back."

After accepting Lindy back into ARC, Allen was accused of "hijacking addicts." The competition for public funds is getting fiercer and an addict with a chance to make it means better statistics. They are in demand.

Flagg thinks about something else as Allen goes on. "I don't believe you people realized that this is one of the few programs that has no political ties. There are a whole lot of organizations that wish they could close this thing down. It's a sore spot, because of the fact that I refuse to accept political ties. The only thing that keeps it going is the fact that they can see some ex-addicts on the staff and that every now and then they can see somebody who really changed.

"Now, I'm in a helluva fix if I'm fightin' against that structure and fightin' against you too."

There are many structures—Federal, state, city, church-affiliated and private—each with a somewhat different philosophy. They call their group sessions Synanons, Encounters, Marathons, or just plain therapy. ARC, like Dr. Ramirez's Phoenix House, is located right in the middle of the problem. Dope is just around the corner. In Allen's case, Harlem is central to the premise.

Allen is interested in improving his own streets and wants his graduates back in them as examples. What good is it to rehabilitate some dude away from his roots? At some point, after he has been doing well, he'll want to return. He could stay away for twenty years but Harlem is home, like it or not, and Allen hasn't helped him at all unless he's armed for it. There is no point turning dope fiends into expatriates.

After having been isolated in a plush Synanon or Daytop

retreat for three years, the shock of the city can be overwhelming. Synanon is overtly uninterested in the problem. "We are not in the addicts rehabilitation business," they say. "We are in the utopian society business. Why send the junkies back into the streets? Look how screwed-up the streets are. There is another way. We will build our own streets." They are buying land, moving their program in that direction.

Since every junkie applying is a potential life-time member, Synanon screens them carefully. It has been said that one must contribute as much as a thousand dollars in order to be admitted, although the Synanon people deny this. They say, "Sure we want money if your family has it. If you had cancer, you'd find a way to pay the hospital bills, wouldn't you?" They say the addict must have motivation or it will never work. So they make him return for interview after interview, screening after screening, before a decision is made.

Daytop, formed when David Daitch left his post as Synanon director after a squabble over their inflexibility, is a bit looser. Unlike Synanon, they will accept funds from the Establishment; from Ramirez for example. As a link between the program and reentry, they have set up SPAN, a sort of decompression chamber. Before graduation, the Daytop resident must work at one of these neighborhood addict service centers while still in residence at the Staten Island plant.

You may have remarked the business terminology. This is a business—and becoming an industry. Synanon, for example, is the largest distributor of advertising specialties west of Chicago, so they brag. And if you don't believe dope fiends can sell, just pull into a Synanon gas station in Santa Monica. I would hate to own one across the street. The cats swarm over you; cleaning, filling, checking, and smiling as if their life depended on it.

Rehabilitated dope fiends are a new breed, only a decade

old. It is clearly the result of the new techniques evolved by Synanon, Ramirez (in Puerto Rico), James Allen, and a few other people like them in the late fifties. Allen, by the way, did not learn about Synanon until he was well on his own way.

The members of the new breed all have something in common: dedication, a certain messianic fervor. They are intensely loyal to their own program and quite vocal in criticizing everybody else. By far the worst are Synanon graduates.

Chester Stern, who runs their New York office—an elegant townhouse on Riverside Drive—is a fine example. I knew Chester slightly when he was a greasy junkie from Brooklyn. He could hustle and con with the best of them. My main memory of Chester is striding down Broadway, his trumpet bag under his arm, leaning forward, scurrying to some urgent appointment. I used to wonder why Chester was always borrowing money and, wanting so much to be accepted by the real beboppers, one of whom I assumed Chester was, I was usually good for a dollar or so at the age of sixteen. Chester was a classic dope fiend. Now that he is a clean, high-powered, efficient executive, I'm not sure which Chester Stern I prefer.

I spent an hour with him in his office, which is large, contains the latest *Business Week* hardware, and has a nice view of the Hudson River. I have also seen him on two television talk shows and so have now heard the same spiel three times.

Handing me a ball-point with "Synanon" imprinted on the clip, he starts: "Synanon is a private foundation supported by subscriptions and our various enterprises. We have no political ties. There are over nine hundred residents in nine Synanon houses. There have been over a hundred marriage ceremonies performed at Synanon and one hundred and fifty children go to our school in Santa Monica, which is fully accredited, incidentally. Our game clubs are not limited to addicts. There are over two thousand active members from all walks of life playing the Synanon game." He hands me a brochure.

Chester's for-the-record personality is reminiscent of Richard Nixon. No matter how hard he tries, he just can't pull off a loose, relaxed manner and he tries too hard. Chester is a politician: "It has been said that Synanon is plush. Yes, we are plush. We want to show the addict—from Harlem, for example—that there is a better way to live. We are also called clubby. If so, everyone in Synanon belongs to the same one, regardless of age, race, religion, sex, or economic status. We are helped by many prominent people in the community who are convinced [some say brainwashed], that our method is the only way and they too belong to the Synanon 'club.' This has the added benefit of giving the resident an opportunity to meet people who can help him after he graduates."

Synanon is integrated, it is true. However, since they are more selective than other programs, and money *does* help, they exclude a priori some ghetto junkies. They wind up with people who have generally less outside pressures on them, a factor conveniently overlooked when they quote statistics.

According to Chester, there is little doubt who is best. You are all fools for not seeing it. He will avoid statistics but when pressed, flippantly gives ninety-seven percent as their rate of success; an impossible figure. Pressed further, he will insist on it although one soon begins to suspect that this figure is based on graduates only. Those screened out in front and any splitees in process have been conveniently discounted.

And even if you accept his figure, the question remains why practically all Synanon graduates appear to be hooked on Synanon. One exception is Zev Putterman who, at the time of this writing, is the producer of the Les Crane television show and who now dresses in three-piece suits and looks like a young Henry Fonda. He is loose and smiles and talks about Synanon with some degree of objectivity.

He recalls the time when David Daitch and James Allen visited the Synanon Westport Connecticut house and wouldn't be admitted. Zev had been transferred there, much like a corporate executive, after some promotions up the Santa Monica hierarchy. "We had a policy," he says, "of not admitting anybody who had cleaned himself up. That could be very destructive, an excuse to split for somebody who isn't secure enough yet. 'If that guy can do it, so can I. I'm getting out of here.' "

That makes sense. But, when Synanon people talk about others in their industry, they tend to sound like Engine Charlie Wilson. Whether or not the accusations against Synanon are true, Zev says, "Look at what it has done for me. You remember what a bum I used to be." He's right: that's all the whole thing is supposed to be about.

James Allen will say honestly, "Nobody has figured out a way to get the addict back out on the street. We know how to detoxify an addict and we know how to keep a reasonable percentage of them clean while they are still residing in a program, but getting them back into society is still difficult. I can't tell you what percentage of success we've had, partly because we haven't had the funds to keep accurate records until recently, but mostly because all of the programs are too new. Who is to say when a man is out of danger. I can only put my fingers on but sixteen guys—and I refuse to make a wild guess. You know, a guy looked good last night and as far as I am concerned he is rehabilitated. But I don't know what the hell he's doing right now. Six months from now I suspect that I will be able to answer that more accurately because with the state money we will have—for the first time—somebody here to keep accurate records."

The money on the way from NACC (the state) is to support and expand the ARC program exactly as it is. There is no obligation to conform to anybody else's theories, good or bad, as with OCAP (Ramirez). The theory of "different strokes for different blokes" is essential to Allen's program.

Apparently the right stroke hasn't been found for Flagg, however, because he's thinking about the Man on 26th Street. The meeting had gone against him. He will not be able to leave the house for thirty days, except on official business or to go to church. There is a dry taste in his mouth.

10

Some Good Stuff

A DRAMA IN ONE ACT

The cast:

Mr. Glenn Mr. Houston Mr. Stokes Mr. Cole (X) Mr. McCarthy	Inactive dope fiends
Miss Lincoln Mr. Washington Mr. Roosevelt	Dope fiends
Mrs. Kosof	A social worker

Bill Glenn is standing by a blackboard in the unadorned therapy room. Ten programmers sit in a semicircle, facing him. The curtainless windows are open to let in mild Fall air and the howling of dogs. There are ashtrays and coffee containers on the unpainted floor. Mr. Glenn removes his glasses and waves them for emphasis. His diction, like his appearance, is neat and unaffected.

Mr. Glenn: I have been wondering, ever since I've been off drugs—and I used to wonder while I was using drugs—why do people say, "once an addict, always an addict"? I have a pet theory.

I used drugs for sixteen years. During those sixteen years I tried very very hard to get away from stuff. I had a measure of success as far as a job was concerned and I didn't really want for anything. I was living with my brother who was pretty well-to-do and things were running along smoothly. And yet I went back to dope. I really can't understand it, not completely.

If anybody has used drugs for five years or more, he's tried to get away at one time or another. Why did you go back, Mr. Houston?

Mr. Houston: I think it is because I was still making negative decisions. It's a matter of what else you do, what other outside surroundings have you picked. I kicked the drug habit itself, but I still had the habits I had when using drugs. Those are the habits which you must control. For example, I stopped using drugs, but I kept stealing. Kept right on stealing. And I went back to drugs eventually. You see, stopping using drugs—that wasn't enough. I know this guy that stopped using drugs, but started selling drugs. He wound up in the penitentiary anyway. So stopping isn't enough. You've got to stop the drug *habits,* you understand. I feel you have got to break all of those bad habits which you acquired while you were addicted.

Mr. Glenn: Yes. Mr. Houston and I share the same opinion. It's our contention that you can't just kick the habit physically. This is nothing. You have only begun to solve what is troubling you. Stopping shooting drugs is only the very beginning. Then, and only then are you starting to kick your habit. Just like Mr. Houston said, the "habits": plural. For all of our adult lives: ten, fifteen, twenty years as the case may be, all these years we have been doing nothing but negative things. All of us. Thinking negatively. Sleeping negatively. Walking negatively. Talking negatively. Everything we did—in jail and out—was in a negative sense. We didn't do anything positively. We didn't do anything constructive. Our whole concept of morality, all of our values were distorted, twisted, from all these years of constant abuse. And this is why I honestly feel it is so difficult for us to really stay away from drugs. Because once we get away from dope physically, we forget it. We say, well that's it. I'm not a junkie. I'm not a dope fiend any more. Well this is not so. You are just an inactive dope fiend. That's all you are. This is all you are until you complete the process, and that takes quite a while, a long time, a very difficult, a very lonely and sometimes a very heartbreaking process.

You know, I haven't used any drugs for well over three years now. But for the entire first year—now dig this, talking about habits. I wasn't shooting any drugs. I wasn't smoking any reefer. I wasn't doing anything as far as drugs were concerned. But there was one habit I just couldn't kick—it took me almost a year to kick it. Walking down the street, any time, I don't care where I was going, walking down the street I could not walk past an automobile without looking in it, seeing if there was something in the back seat—a camera, a radio, anything—to steal. For sixteen years, any time I'd walk anywhere I'd be looking for some sting, you know that. I don't care if you've got a thousand dollars in your pocket, if you see a typewriter or something in a car that's open, you're going to snatch it and go. Right? It's a habit. And for a whole year, you know what I used to have to do? I really did this. When I went out in the street, I used to force myself to walk up as close to the wall as I possibly could. So if I did look I couldn't see anything. I'm not jiving you. I'm not trying to dramatize. I'm telling you a fact about me.

Now I can walk down the street and I don't even know there's a car by the sidewalk. But before I just could not under any circumstances—coming from work, walking with my wife, going to church, I don't care what it was—keep from looking. I wouldn't have taken anything out of one of those cars if you had paid me to do it, but I still held on to that habit from when I was using dope.

A habit. Only one. There were hundreds of other habits I had to kick. Like all of us do. When I was using stuff, I used to walk down the street and look in a store at a suit. I'd never even visualize how that suit would look on me. When I saw that suit, the price—a hundred and fifty dollars, whatever it might have been—I was thinking, man, if I had that I could get me ten bags. That's what that suit meant to me. I could get me a half a piece with that one. Look at that boss television set—if I had that I'd be straight for the weekend.

Values didn't mean anything. My conversation started with five dollars. Under five dollars was very unimportant. It didn't mean a thing. Because that's what a bag of stuff costs. See, when a guy would come to me and talk about a dollar, I'd say go away. What are you talking about a dollar? But my thoughts were always on a five-dollar level or more. I didn't even realize that I could take a dollar and ride back and forth from work for three or four days. Twenty cents is a subway fare. What? Twenty cents? If I wanted to get in the subway I'd go under the turnstile. These are habits that you have to kick.

Here is another thing; the way you talk. You get into a habit of dope-fiend talk. Ten, fifteen, sixteen years, you talk like a dope fiend. Like, "Hey man, what's happenin'? Yeah man, like, who's got the stuff, man?" All of a sudden your voice isn't normal any more. You become pretentious. "Yeah. Crazy." It becomes a habit. And you find a lot of people still talk that way today because they think it's slick. They haven't kicked that part of the habit yet. And you know something? Every one—without any exceptions—who holds on to any of these habits, sooner or later goes back to dope. Every one.

This is what I think. Mr. McCarthy. How do you feel? What is the reason, in your opinion?

Mr. McCarthy: I can only speak for myself. I wasn't ready. I was still using some coke, I smoked some reefer, I did this for a couple of months. And I did a little stealing. I was not ready. I am ready now. I know this because the girl I was with was using stuff and I used it twice, with her. I eliminated that by getting rid of her because I could not keep looking at her taking off. She was not going to come to my program and I definitely was not going to hers. So I said, "The only thing we can do is separate." She said, "You're not fooling around this time, are you?" I said, "No baby. It's all over." Because . . . I am tired. Kicking is hard for me. I'm in trouble. I have less now than I ever had. . . .

Mr. Glenn: I disagree. I think that you have more.

Mr. McCarthy: I mean less financially.

Mr. Glenn: Success is not measured in finances, material things, I know so many unhappy, discontented people who have all the money they know what to do with. Success is not measured in material things. Some of the most successful, the richest, people I know are unsuccessful human beings. No, baby . . . it's good to have money and I wish I had as much as I could get my hands on. But this is not my aim in life, to get material things. Because if you are going to measure success by the material things in life, you are never going to be successful. You can never get as much as you really want. Never. You will go on and on and on until you drop dead from exhaustion, making money.

I'm not down on money. Don't get me wrong. I'm not down on having a nice home and a nice car, expensive clothes. I like these things. But these are not criterias of success. As a human being. You can be just as happy being neat and clean, wearing eight-dollar pants or a fifteen-dollar sweater, a dollar-and-a-half shirt. And be just as happy as a guy who walks in here with a five-hundred-dollar suit. Happier really, because he might be worrying about somebody beating him for that suit, sticking him up or something. I'm not worried about anybody taking anything I've got.

What kind of person am I? That's my measurement of success. When you have peace of mind, this is what success really is, the success in being a human being. A person. If you have some friends, people who like you and who you like, who worry about you when you get sick, come and see you or send you a card, that is a successful thing.

Lucky Luciano had a lot of money, but he couldn't even walk down the street without fifty people around him. Is that successful? The guy out here dealin' in kilos and things. What do you call him, a success? He's ducking every cop that he sees. He's afraid. He's probably got ulcers and he's drinking himself to death and he's staying up all night—he's not a success. Mr. Washington. What do you think? Why do you think most people can't seem to stay away from dope?

Mr. Washington: I don't know. I have tried. Tried hard. In fact I tried so hard that I had two jobs. But I wasn't ready for it. I have searched, double-searched and researched, but I can't find the answer. I'm tired. Getting old and tired of running, of snatching, dragging, giving money away for what? Nothing. I don't even get high no more. I just shoot dope to keep from getting sick.

Mr. Glenn: Mr. Roosevelt. What do you think?

Mr. Roosevelt: I have tried myself. I've tried. I even sold dope without using any—for almost a year. But then, I've gone back and used it again. I end up going back to dope. I don't know why.

Mr. Glenn: Why is it so difficult to readjust? Why is it so difficult to get away? We know about all the degrading things we must do and undergo. We know this. If we shoot dope, we're going to jail. We know that if we shoot dope, sooner or later we're going to be sleeping on a roof or in a basement.

We know that when we shoot dope, we aren't going to have any time for friends. Seventy-five percent of the time we are going to be feeling miserable. We have to go out and steal the money to get that fix, to feel what we call good. We know all of this, after using drugs ten or fifteen years. We know this. Who could want this way of life? When a person shoots dope, he's telling me that he likes to go to jail, to sleep in basements, he likes to steal, likes to have people hate him. That's exactly what he's saying. No normal human being likes these things. Yet, he knows that this is exactly what is going to happen. He knows this. It's not maybe, he hasn't been told it's going to happen, he didn't read about it or see it in a movie or on TV, he *knows* from his own experience that this is going to happen. If you shoot that dope there is only one thing that can possibly happen to you. Yet, most of us go back and shoot that dope. Why?

Being an ex-addict is a twenty-four hour a day, seven day a week job, three hundred and sixty-five days a year. You work at it. You work at it by degrees. You acquire the ability to stand up and argue with somebody, to reason out an argument without resorting to a punch in the nose or getting angry or not speaking any more.

When you start giving up drugs you've got to force yourself to do things you don't really want to. Constructive things. You've got to force yourself to do them. And then there comes a time when you can just do these things normally. You can even refuse, normally.

Stop and think about some of the things you do and say during the course of the day. Seriously think about them. Stop really. And I'll bet you'll say, "How can I be so stupid? How can I have been so childish? That don't make any sense. That's the way a kid would react." You take a piece of candy from a kid, he starts to scream. You've done the same thing a thousand times.

I assume you all want to stay away from dope. I don't know anybody who really wants to stay on dope. I know a lot of people who are jiving. But they're jiving themselves, that's all. Miss Lincoln, when is the last time that you had some dope?

Miss Lincoln: The last time? Do you mean from a doctor?

Mr. Glenn: I mean the last time, however you want.

Miss Lincoln: Er . . . uh . . . forty-nine days.

Mr. Glenn: Forty-nine days! That must have been some *good* stuff.

Miss Lincoln: Why do you say that?

Mr. Glenn: When you say doctor, do you mean a doctor gave you something?

Miss Lincoln: Yes. He gave me Malada, Melanga . . . I can't pronounce it. It's like . . . what do you call it?

(Several voices: Dilaudit?)

Miss Lincoln: Yeah. That's right. Dilaudit.

Mr. Glenn: When did you start using dope?

Miss Lincoln: Start? Me? . . . 1954. Of course I didn't start completely then. It was a few years later. I've been using stuff off and on since then. I never did use no goof balls, though. I've been very fortunate. I've never had to sleep in no cellars or on no roofs. Every time I'd get into a position like that, I'd always check into a hospital. I'd never let myself get greasy. I've also always been fortunate because I've had relatives who have been in the position to help me out, take me in and . . . you know . . . I'd never have to be in the gutter. Then, too, I've always had good friends . . . men friends . . . who, they wouldn't pay me or nothin', understand. But they was nice to me.

I'm puzzled, though. Why did you pick me to ask when the last time was?

Mr. Glenn: What reason do you think I had for asking you?

Miss Lincoln: I don't know. It just puzzled me, that's all. . . . This time, I've been off since . . . uh . . . forty-nine days and . . . uh . . . I haven't been using nothing. That's the truth. 'Cause if I make my mind up to do something, I do it. And I'm very touchy. I don't like for nobody to accuse me of having—

Mr. Glenn: Nobody's accusing you of anything. . . .

Miss Lincoln: —Because the people who know me, they ain't ever saw me out there greasy . . . if I'm getting real bad I go to a hospital and if they ain't got any room I act crazy and they put me in the psycho. But I get my habit kicked. I come out. I work for a while. I've been fortunate. I've always worked. I always kept myself up good. And whenever I got busted, my brother-in-law would come right up and get me out. Get me out on bail. I've always been fortunate. . . .

Mr. Glenn: Fortunate? That's the word I heard. Fortunate. I guess it depends on what a person calls fortunate. I think it was very unfortunate.

Miss Lincoln: When's the last time you had a drink?

Mr. Glenn: A drink? What's today . . . Friday? Last Saturday.

Miss Lincoln: You know why I ask that? Because you said earlier that you didn't drink or anything any more.

Mr. Glenn: No, no. If I said that, I most certainly told you a lie—or you completely misunderstood me. No, no. I said I didn't use any kind of drugs. I wouldn't tell anybody that I don't take a drink occasionally. When I say occasionally, that means once in two, or maybe three weeks.

Miss Lincoln: I find that if you're trying to get off drugs, it helps to take a little drink to tide you over the rough spots. Or to smoke a little reefer now and then to keep away that urge . . . you know. I don't care who you are—that helps to get it off your mind.

Mr. Glenn: I agree with you. You know, I agree with that more than with anything that anybody else said here today. A hundred percent I agree with you.

Miss Lincoln: Why?

Mr. Glenn: Because what you really said is that years of using dope makes you nothing, that being a dope fiend you can't do anything normal, that after you get off dope, you've got to resort to some sort of negative something to replace the other. I agree with that. One hundred percent. And this is why you are always going to be a dope fiend unless you stop clinging to that way of life.

Miss Lincoln: Well I need *something,* you know . . . it's not easy, and I was never a . . .

Mr. Glenn: Yes. I agree with you. Now don't get me wrong. You will be a *clean* drug addict. Not a dirty, greasy, no good junkie; just a clean dope fiend. . . .

(Miss Lincoln leaves, crying. Mrs. Kosof follows her.) . . . We've got a lot to learn, an awful lot to learn.

(Watches Miss Lincoln and Mrs. Kosof go out.)

We walked out of society. We ostracized ourselves from what we call the square world. They didn't put us out. We ran away. We started shooting dope, and stealing and lying and cheating and going in and out of jail. And so now we got tired of doing all these things—we say. If we had only stolen from drug addicts, only cheated other drug addicts, this would be okay. Then I could go back to society and say I've never done anything to you. The only people I ever hurt was myself and some other dope fiends. But this is not true. We *harmed* the same people that we are begging to re-accept us. We're begging them to trust us. I stole everything you had and worked twenty years for—I stole it all from you in one night. But now I no longer use drugs so please, love me. This is exactly what we're saying.

We are begging. We are pleading. Please accept me. And

they are saying to us, "All right, prove yourself. I don't owe you a thing." That's what society is telling us. "I don't owe you anything. You owe me. Now you come and you prove to me that you are worthy of my acceptance and then maybe, and only maybe, after a period of years will I really accept you completely. Only maybe."

Sooner or later, they will accept you—but not on the basis of what you say. They are not going to even listen to us any more, because we have proven that we are a bunch of liars and cheaters. I've gone to society a thousand times and told so many lies and got what I could and then turned my back and went away. I don't expect them to accept me simply because I *say* that I'm not shooting any dope. They don't owe me a thing.

Now the sooner you learn that and recognize that, the better off you'll be. Because you and I made them say those things about you. I cheated them, I stole, I killed—not literally killed, but I killed the love that people had for me, the respect that people had for me. I did it. Now I'm pleading with them. On my knees. "Please," I'm pleading with them. "Please take me back." But not only am I pleading, I'm doing something about it. I'm proving it to them. And I'll go on proving it until sooner or later—maybe after five or ten or fifteen years—they'll all open their doors and say okay, come on back in, you are once again a part of us. You've proven yourself. But I don't expect it in two, three, or six months—or five years, for that matter. They'll accept you sooner or later if you keep proving it. . . .

(Mrs. Kosof returns to her chair.)

. . . What Miss Lincoln said was simply a defense for her old way of life. We all recognize this . . . I allowed it to go on, because I want everybody to see and hear . . . she's *defending* her way of life. She is "fortunate." She used the word fortunate. How can an addict use that word? Don't be ridiculous. There is no such word as "fortunate" in a dope addict's life. I don't care if he gets a kilo of dope every day. You aren't fortunate. You are the most unfortunate human being that God ever created. Are you fortunate because you can con people and prove you're a big phony?

And don't condemn squares. I would pay attention to so-called squares if I were you. If there's a person who has never used any dope, I'd listen to that person pretty carefully. See what he has to say. Why didn't you use dope? Why didn't you turn out to be a junkie? We have the same education, you know. I'm not illiterate, neither are you. I have a reasonable amount of intelligence, so do you. But I was a dope fiend. Why weren't you? There's the possibility that a square could tell me something. I'll listen. And I'll use everything that I possibly can—from *anybody*—who is not using dope. Sooner or later I'm going to come up with the thing that's going to keep me from using dope. . . . Yes, Mr. Houston.

Mr. Houston: I'd like to say something about that girl—Miss Lincoln. She should never have gotten up those stairs. Now it wasn't her fault. When she comes in she's supposed to sign the book and we don't have any blind people working on the desk. They should stop her and ask the time, the weather—talk to her. Something. But she got up here and her feelings were hurt. She got insulted. She knows what Mr. Glenn was saying is right. But the point is, it wasn't necessary. She shouldn't have even gotten to the stairs. The person on the desk should have stopped her. If you've got a job to do, you should do it right. She should never have gotten past signing that book.

Mr. Glenn: I did not want her to leave for a very good reason—I saw where she was at, you know. She was under the influence of drugs and we all know this. I wanted us to hear ourselves: yourself. You were listening to you. I was listening to me. Now you dig how ridiculous she was, how stupid her reasoning was? The greatest thing that ever happened to her was that she could get all the drugs she wanted. This is a very logical thing for a drug addict to think of.

Mrs. Kosof: Mr. Houston, she was let up for a considered reason. Mr. Feimster felt that this could do her a lot of good. She's talking to him now. She's crying. This is what we wanted to happen. This was exactly what was designed to happen. To crack her. Because if she doesn't get past the desk and she goes back out there, you know where she's going. Maybe this little bit of therapy . . . call it whatever it is . . . will just be the last straw. This may be the thing which will get her to realize that she's jiving, that she's lying. Yes. I know the rules, and I know what you're saying. You're right. But in this particular case, we made an exception because we felt that this could do her a lot of good. And I think that it has helped. It may not be obvious right now that it's helped—she's crying and very upset—but tomorrow or next week this may have helped. She will think twice before she comes under the influence of drugs again.

Mr. Houston: She might think twice about even coming back at all.

Mrs. Kosof: I doubt it. Maybe she won't come back for two weeks. It may take her two months. But the odds are she will come back.

Mr. Houston: In the course of that two months she may take one shot too many.

Mrs. Kosof: But she will take one shot too many regardless.

Mr. Houston: She could have been taken around to Mr. Feimster.

Mrs. Kosof: She is talking to Mr. Feimster . . .

Mr. Houston: I think that talking to someone like that in

a group, the way she was spoken to, is very harmful. She is a very emotional person. She might come back tomorrow, but more likely she'll get a fix.

Mrs. Kosof: You may very well be right. But I don't think so. She didn't go outside. She stopped. She put her coat on the bannister. If she wanted to leave, she would have just gone right on out. But she didn't leave.

Mr. Glenn: You both have a point. This is one of those things we will never know. Or at least until time proves it. I think it helped her really. Even though she is under the influence of drugs, she knows she's jiving. That crying was only part of her game. She was milking us for sympathy. We know that. That's not important. She's crying because she couldn't get us to sympathize. I feel this way, that no matter what happens to her out there, if she honestly wants help, she'll be back. I don't think that, even in the smaller sense, the experience destroyed her. She knows that she was wrong. When she wakes up and finally admits it, then she'll come back.

Not only that. It helped everybody else sitting here. You looked in a mirror, sitting right there in that chair. This is me. There I am. And you began to be frightened. I know I did. Frightened of myself. Because there I sat trying to play the game. Falsely crying and defending my way of life. There I sat looking at me. I sat on the outside and saw myself. Me. And I don't think it will hurt her. There was nothing said to her that wasn't true, that she knows is true. I don't think anybody degraded her to the point where she was any less of a woman than she was when she came in because she was just a baby sitting there. She wasn't a human being because she treats herself as less than a human being. Our arguing with her, our saying that we know what she is saying is a lot of baloney, this has to help her.

Mr. Houston: In front of a room full of people? She should have been spoken to in private.

Mr. Stokes: As long as that woman sat there and nodded and kept her mouth shut, nobody would have bothered her. If she didn't play on the intelligence of the entire group by sitting there and saying that a shot of delaudit lasts from Saturday to Friday. Are we all imbeciles because we stopped using drugs? We haven't blown our minds because we have stopped using narcotics.

Mr. Houston: But I feel this way. That girl didn't break no program rules. The program broke the rules—by letting her come up here.

Mr. Stokes: When she came to the desk, she broke a rule. She is not supposed to come to the Center high.

Mr. Houston: That man's job down there was to enforce the rules. That's all I'm saying. That's what he is getting paid to do. I feel that he should have done it. The girl should not have been exploited.

Mr. Stokes: She wasn't exploited.

Mr. Houston: Oh yes she was.

Mr. Glenn: Please, please . . . hold it. This debate could go on all this afternoon and into tomorrow. I respect both opinions and I can see value in both of them. It's just a matter of what came first, the chicken or the egg. I personally believe that there was no harm done. And a good purpose was served if there was, a sacrifice of one to save many. I think that we, as ex-addicts, should think of this on another level. That we will never put ourselves in this position. If she wants help, she'll get it. Don't worry about her. Let's worry about ourselves, that we won't put ourselves in the same position any more. It's good to have concern for people, but most of our concern should be centered around ourselves. Just remember what this sign up here says. . . .

We don't use stuff!

"we must be doing
something right"

. . . Our time is up. Thank you.

From *New Life* (ARC newsletter):

SLAVERY OR FREEDOM

"OH GOD", free me from those cold steel needles and mountains of white powder that have me shackled in space::::I can't breathe, I can't see, I can't hear.-----Give me death--give me life--give me freedom. I cannot live yet I cannot die--for I am a slave . . . "Oh God", free me from these cold steel needles******and mountains of white powder:::::::::::::::::::

This is the cry of a slave, a living, walking dead man----a drug addict************

Since the beginning of time man has been begging, praying, fighting, dying to be freed from the bondage of slavery. Man has been enslaved by hate, enslaved by fear, enslaved by love, and enslaved by man, but man has always fought and died to be free........

It's incredulous to believe that in this modern age of atomic energy, of guided missels, of trips to the moon, that there are thousands of men and women who are begging, fighting, praying, dying to be slaves.

I thought I was slick::::I didn't know what I was doing:::I wanted to be with the In-Crowd::: my home life was very unhappy:::I was very poor . . . These are but a few of the excuses given by the drug addict for his first step into the bowels of hell----his self imposed slavery.

These are only excuses, for there is no valid reason that I can give for my voluntary exile from humanity . . . Emotional immaturity, ignorance, social insecurity, a false feeling of inferiority, a lack of faith in God, and myself---these too, I have called reasons. But, whatever the excuse, (or reason if you prefer) once I have taken this step into slavery why can't I or why don't I fight to free myself? Is it because of my new masters, "the needle and the powder", have so completely enslaved my body, my soul, my mind, that I no longer have the physical, the spiritual, the mental ability to reason and act for myself???? If this be true, then I am doomed to an eternity of slavery . . . "But Wait"::: Maybe there is a way out::::: If I can't do it alone, then maybe I can if someone will help me;;; "But Who"???? Whom can I turn to for help in freeing me from these shackles??? "God??" Will God help me????? a lowly, despised, dirty, disbelieving drug addict????"Yes" "Yes", that's the answer----I can ask God;;;;;;No,,,I won;t ask him, I'll plead with him, I'll beg him, I'll pray to him---- "Oh how I'll pray to him-----Oh God, free me from these cold steel needles**********and mountains of white powder...............

WILLIAM (BILL) GLENN

11
Jesus Among the Rednecks

It is possible that many
people take heroin because
they sense unconsciously that
if they did not, they would
be likely to commit murder,
get cancer or turn homosexual.

NORMAN MAILER
The Presidential Papers

". . . or die of the ugliness," Mailer might have added about Harlem dope fiends. At a young age, junk is quite a discovery: something more than a dollar and a quarter an hour. It is so readily available that any kid with spunk and some change is bound to try it. Who likes to contemplate living in garbage and sweeping up men's rooms for the rest of his life? Junk solves that problem for a while.

Jesus Larí grew up poorly in East Harlem. He is tall, slender, and speaks with a slightly lisped genteel Southern drawl, a bit like Tennessee Williams. He doesn't look Puerto Rican.

Jesus' father was bohemian, a pimp, a revolutionary, and a poet, who studied in Italy and drank himself to death in 1952. Mrs. Larí, a nurse, supported Mr. Larí and their two children by performing abortions. She bought the old man two bars which he lost. She worked from nine in the morning until seven at night, always had three or four hundred dollars in her pocket and contributed a good share of it to the church.

For three years now Jesus has been off stuff; and on staff for one. Since he would like to be a writer, and is naturally open and gregarious, he was one of my first friends up there.

Jesus has a block. Pick your cop-out, he has it. I'm too busy this week. I just can't seem to decide what I want to write about. Maybe I should take a course in creative writing first. The neighbors complain if I type late at night. Like that.

Doing bits in jails and hospitals, Jesus has written some poems, many letters and fragments which he asked me to look at. We made a date at my place one Tuesday night. He was right on time.

"Hey, this is nice," he said. "So this is what a loft looks like? It's a great life, being a writer, isn't it?"

I showed him around and we listened to records for a while. After coffee, I asked to see the pieces—he had a portfolio which I had assumed contained them. But no, he hadn't been able to find them. They must be packed away someplace. He would dig them out sometime next week.

I was annoyed and it probably showed. "Don't you see what you are doing?" I asked him. Thinking how he was wasting my time, about to go on like that, I pulled myself up. No amount of prodding would work until he was ready anyway. And I realized my reaction was selfish. After all the pep talks I'd given him, I was bugged—insulted, even—at his continued negative response. Which was ridiculous.

Because of Jesus, I had turned down an invitation from some friend of mine to fall by their recording session at a small studio a few blocks away. Now I suggested going over there.

In Los Angeles, pop groups build their own studios. Bright fluorescents, old coffee containers, too much chrome, and union help ("Don't touch that microphone!") are no longer unavoidable, cutting an album. Why put up with mass production? Why be in public when you can afford privacy?

That kind of thing is generally too expensive in New York, real estate values being where they are. But Hall's is close. One flight up in a loft neighborhood which is deserted at night, Hall's is also two locked doors from the street. The pressed tin ceiling is baffled with egg cartons. Lights are low. There are plenty of couches and easy chairs. Photographs of Mama Cass, Billie Holiday, Paul McCartney, and Charlie Parker decorate the walls. There are no unwanted visitors.

My friends call themselves The Rednecks. They are all from the Deep South and, although white, play a rhythm and blues, down home, soulful country style of rock and roll. They have quite a bit of hippy in them and Polly, the lead singer, was rolling grass as we arrived.

I admit to a little panic. Would Jesus take a few pokes and lickety-split go out, take off, and get strung out again? But it would be awkward to leave so soon. I wondered how he would react. Polly passed me a lit joint.

Jesus was busy digging the band. I leaned over, nudging his arm to get his attention. I offered it to him. "What?" he said. ". . . Oh, no. Thanks Mike but I don't feel like it." He was cool as can be.

For those readers who are critical of what they consider to be an irresponsible act on my part, let me say I do not completely agree with Mr. Allen on the subject of marijuana. Pot doesn't lead to heroin any more inevitably than beer to alcoholism. It is the milieu—specifically the ghetto in this case—which does it, in conjunction with certain character disorders I felt strongly Jesus no longer had.

Marijuana means something else to a junkie. Dope fiends must be very careful of it just as an alcoholic with that first fatal glass of beer. I believe, along with Mr. Allen, in "different strokes for different blokes," and Jesus is very much a person who deserves his own stroke.

In any event he was perfect. There was a warm smile on his face as he said, "Isn't that chick beautiful? Look at her."

Polly was on the piano bench, her long bangs covering half her face, beads and bells swinging back and forth as she rolled another joint, belting a song at the same time.

Jesus settled into his chair, grooving. . . .

He always got busted in May; looked forward to it. The Joint wasn't such a bad place anyway—he could clean up, eat well for a change, do some reading—especially on Hart's Island, while it was open. He loved sitting by the water watching the sailboats, writing poems. It was kind of like a vacation; the only situation under which he and his friends were in any position to relate to each other. Amazing, the kind of love they had, how beautiful they were off dope.

The Federal penitentiary in Lewisburg, Pennsylvania, was no vacation, though. (Jesus had been caught passing bad checks.) Towards the end of a three-year stretch, disgusted with life, moody, restless, he cried almost every day. It had always been his philosophy to make time serve him, serving time, but he no longer had the self-control. Several months since he last played his guitar, he had also given up taking correspondence courses.

It seemed like ninety percent of the population was homosexual. The way those guys romped around, played with each other, and made love at night, you would think they were women. Jesus wanted a woman badly. Four weeks before his release he found himself hard over a guy in the shower room. Looking at his ass—it was so smooth, so tight, and with such a nice little shape to it—he imagined it female. He barely managed those four weeks.

Having a girl to go back to helped. He kept thinking about her, his own woman waiting for him.

They had met at the Lexington, Kentucky, railroad station. Waiting for the train home, he saw five girls get out of a car to make the same train. They all looked as healthy as girls do leaving K. Y. The guys with Jesus started sizing up the girls and vice versa. It is an eighteen-hour ride to New York.

By train time, everybody had paired off except Jesus and a Jewish-looking girl. He tasted from a jug until the alcohol was ready to speak, then motioned her over. She was overjoyed, just beaming. They talked about the music they liked—Dave Brubeck, Johnny Mathis, Frank Sinatra—and hit it right off. They talked almost the whole way.

Reaching New York, they scored right away and made love, partying for two days in a midtown hotel. Jesus figured that was that. It was over, a nice scene but over. He did not plan to call her again. But as he wandered around town the next day, which was sunny and mild, he began thinking about her. He had her number. She said come on by. They bought more dope and partied some more until the funds were exhausted two weeks later.

Now the party ended. Jesus hinted first—he started it, he admits it now. He knew she'd done it before, hustle her ass. She went out early one evening. He went to his mother's, where he was technically living. About midnight, the phone rang. "Honey," she said, "I have fifty dollars but I think I can get more. Should I?"

"By all means, get more," Jesus said.

"But I'm not too sure. . . ."

"About what?"

"There's a guy right outside the phone booth and he wants me to go to his room at the Sheraton. He says there are four more men there and they'll give me twenty dollars each."

"So what's the problem honey?"

"Well, I'm afraid he's the police."

"Check him out," Jesus said. "You've done that before. Look at his shoes. What color are they?"

". . . Brown."

"Doesn't sound like a cop. Talk to him and try to see if he has a gun. You know what to do."

"Okay. Okay, I'll call you back."

Four o'clock that morning the phone rang again, waking him up. "Sweetheart," she said, "I have a hundred and fifty dollars."

Jesus was wide awake. "I'll take a cab and be right down."

They rented a small room on 168th Street and went on that way until Jesus got busted for the checks and sent up to Lewisburg. For three years they wrote each other love letters. His became more romantic with time and he did not notice any change in hers. She was still using but not so much, she said. He would help her kick. The closer his release came the more beautiful he remembered her.

So the shock was fantastic. She was an old woman. Out of her mind on goof balls, thin, blotchy-skinned, wearing rags, she kept kissing him at the bus station. She wanted to go right to a hotel.

She undressed. He couldn't believe it. He had forgotten what dope does to a woman. He couldn't make it.

"You better get dressed and go on home," he said. "I don't feel like it right now. I'll call you later. I'm sorry."

She cried. She needed his help so badly. She borrowed five dollars before leaving.

Jesus vomited. His depression was incredible. He wept. He got on his knees and prayed and prayed. "I'm clean now," he prayed. "I'm clean now, please let me stay clean." It poured out, prayer after prayer. It was almost as if somebody else was praying through him. Finally, around dawn, he fell asleep on the floor.

The next day was like magic. Overnight, all he could think about was God, God, God. He stopped smoking. He fasted. He lost all desire for worldly things. He read the Scriptures endlessly. But the revelation came in his old neighborhood, among the same buildings, seeing the same people doing the same things, leading the same life as always. It was the only scene he knew; it is not a holy scene and he fell.

It was even worse this time. On top of everything else he felt guilty, which resulted in a desire to get busted: punished. He couldn't manage it, not even in May. He couldn't even go to jail this time. He pulled heavier crimes more blatantly. Nothing. By the time a second May came around, he began to think of it as God's work. "He's trying to tell me something," Jesus thought one painful day. "He's telling me I have to do it for myself. I have to get out of here."

He volunteered into Lexington. Recognizing that he was over thirty and not equipped to do anything, he took advantage of an opening in sewage disposal. He had read somewhere that there was a future in that business. The Lexington sewage treatment plant is far removed, way down by the highway, where the cows are; quiet, peaceful, and the birds sing. You see a little tavern across the way.

One by one the other guys checked out, urging Jesus to come north with them. But he waited. This time he wanted to be sure before leaving, this trip to K. Y. would be more than fattening up.

One day in August, down by the cows, a voice said to him —he heard it loud and clear—"It's time to leave. You're cured, I'm telling you it's time to go."

Back in the world, the show soon started. A broad on the train had two bottles of Thunderbird wine. "Let's have a ball, baby," she said. "When we get to New York, I know where to get some dope. I'll be glad to share it with you."

"No, honey," Jesus said. "Don't do that to me. I don't

want no dope. See that Puerto Rican fellow over there? Maybe he wants some dope."

Everything seemed beautiful in New York, even the view of Twelfth Avenue—Jesus had a temporary job with the United Parcel Service. Events tend to develop a momentum of their own and when one thing goes well, others follow. If you have a success in business, you get nice taxi drivers. When you are in love the subway is less crowded. Since Jesus was off dope he worked in the most pleasant department, the only one in which there was no chaos. The supervisor was Hungarian, cultured, and polite. He knew Jesus was going to night school, tightening up his English. "Bring your books here, if you want," he offered, "maybe I can help you with your studies."

The Hungarian was too polite to give an order. "Mr. Larí," he would say, "if you would be so kind; please take these packages and make sure they are put on the truck . . . thank you." He was even polite saying, "Mr. Larí, I must lay you off now. It's not my doing because I like the way you work and if it was up to me I would not do it. But I will keep your name on file and if a steady position comes up, I would like to call you back."

Jesus temporarily became doorman at Lord and Taylor's department store. An employer wanting value and a half for his payroll dollar should look into ex-dope fiends. Jesus was doubly polite, early, and more diligent than necessary, proving himself. The rich old ladies loved his smiling deference and energy. One took the trouble to commend him to the president who shook his hand and said, "Jesus, you are doing a wonderful job. However, as you know, it is only temporary. . . ."

Lord and Taylor's paid the employment agency fee, gave him a bonus bottle of Scotch and Jesus went away whistling: four hundred dollars' worth of tips in his pocket.

It would be wrong to say he was never tempted. All you need is a little dirt in your life, a little stress and strain which might cause "normal" people to get drunk, and the whole thing can blow up. It can't be done without help. As soon as he heard about the Center, Jesus made it a point to fall by. It began to be a regular thing, hanging out with the brethren, so to speak.

. . . The Rednecks were rehearsing a new tune when we left around two. Although it was a cold and windy night, we stood on a corner talking for a while before saying goodbye. Rather, Jesus talked.

It was a soliloquy. He had had such a beautiful evening—something different. It was so nice watching people who loved to play music. He was going to get with his guitar again. He thanked me. He wanted so badly to write, to tell the stories he knew. He would put aside some time every day. How wonderful it was to be just a guy with normal problems.

From *New Life* (ARC newsletter):

THAT'S OUR MAIN MAN

A quiet, almost heart breaking counsel was being conducted very professionaly by the desk clerk of the ARC. The mother and son sat quietly and listened very attentively to the middle age counselor. There was strained anxiety in the rather young mother's voice--and it all had an aura of serene depth and despair.

. . . A burst of sound came rushing through the street door of the reception room---"Call Greenwich House and get me the address; write it down!" Mr. Allen, the program director, had just begun his day at the Addicts Rehabilitation Center. He strode swiftly past the solemn duo who sat somberly at Mr. Randolph's desk, and proceeded hastily onto the back of the office. "Where's Richard?" he yelled back. Mr. Randolph opened his mouth as if to speak and half turned in his chair, placing one elbow stylishly upon the back rest--thought better of it, and remained silent. Randolph excused himself as he picked up his glasses and proceeded to thumb through a desk calendar, then scribbled the information on a square of a paper. Allen swept back past the young man and his mother, and stood at the desk studying what Randy had handed him. He asked a few concise questions, was answered, and went on to relate very perfunctorily what had to be done during his absence. "Ok . . . I'm late--tell Richard to call me as soon as he can; and to make sure Mr. Fleer gets the information I typed up for him last night." Allen spun, pushed his glasses back on his nose, and gave one more command as he started towards the door.

Before the end of his day, Mr. Allen had made six phone calls from Greenwich House, spoke to a persistent candidate for membership as he drove towards his destination, and returned to the office in time to receive two "trainees" from the State Narcotic Addiction Control Commission.

The director of ARC walks in a fury, and leaves in his wake a stream of sighing staff members who look helplessly up at the sky and proceed to take care of the business at hand. Ultimately, however, in spite of the complex and turbulent personage, the program has a modicum of success which appears to be attainable only by the discipline Mr. Allen has applied to his life, combined with the dedication he also seeks in appointed staff.

Once in his office: Mr. Allen works with an almost mad like intensity which is in direct contrast to his lethargic delivery when making a public speech, or, when holding his daily orientation with new members of the center.

But there's another side to this man so keenly interested in the problem. "All work and no play makes Jack a dull boy." And Mr. Allen emerges out of his office as though he had suddenly became aware of this adage. "Stomp! Stomp." Stomp." " can be heard through the rafters of the ceiling, down the narrow stairs, into the reception room, accompanied with an old religious song that must have been sung during the days Fredrick Douglas had just made his break to freedom. Mr. Allen will sing and stomp noisely around the room, swaying from side to side, then burst into hilarious laughter, adding: "That's a religious song you know; from the old days." The ensuing conversation may be about the days when Allen too, was addicted to drugs. Or he may look around and find someone to make fun of. Or, at other times, he may ease out of his paper-maze office into the recreation room. "You play chess? . . . You? . . . You? . . . C'mon." And when Mr. Allen sits at a chess game; the center can turnover three Banner in full volume; the T.V. can change to color, jump out of the cabinet, and play ping pong with a member. And if one were to inform Mr. Allen of the situation; he's apt to reply: "write it down."

Jesus Larí

12
Poet Laureate of Dope Fiends

Two hundred fifty thousand dollars came through from the state. Morale was high. There was a Ping Pong table in the game room, formerly a storage area, and it had been painted. Lindy's walk was even springier. Nix danced with more than his usual gusto to some new releases coming from the day room. People leaving the afternoon session, just over, all carried clay ashtrays, beads and things they had made up there with newly purchased supplies. Randy was phoning in a bulk grocery order for a change.

A second desk had been added in the reception room and Jesus was sitting there, typing out reports on a brand new portable electric.

"Things have changed since the last time I was here," I said. "That's a groovy typewriter."

"It's hot," he joked. "With all these new people in the program, they just put ten new day-care cases on me. You know we got twenty-eight residents now? It's getting to be utter chaos around this joint. I don't see how I can possibly keep up with the load; I've been counseling all morning. . . . Hey, you want to see something? Look over there."

A guy sitting next to Ike at the front desk was in a good nod. "Mr. Jordan," Ike said, "are you telling me you don't use narcotics?"

Ike looked at us, smiled with a hopeless shrug and shook Mr. Jordan's arm. "Mr. Jordan. . . ."

"I can hear you," Mr. Jordan said, annoyed, scratching himself.

"If you want to come into the rehabilitation program, you will have to take a urine analysis." (A price for the state grant.)

"I'm not an addict," Mr. Jordan said. "I don't know why they sent me over here. I don't use drugs. I told them that."

"You mean you don't have a history of using narcotics?"

"No, not me."

"I was an addict for eighteen years myself. You sure you don't want to retract that statement?"

Mr. Jordan started on another nod. Ike dialed the phone. "Hello. Welfare? Did you send a guy over to ARC just now? . . ."

Anna Kosof came in. "Did you hear? We got our money from the state," she said. "It was quite a ceremony. You should have been there. Mr. Pierce himself presented it and a lot of people from the community were there. It was really moving."

Ike hung up, nudged Mr. Jordan, and asked him if he would like ARC to help him get into the hospital.

"Hospital?" he said. "What for? I'm not sick."

"Well, look. You better go back over to the Welfare. There's nothing we can do for you here."

Mr. Jordan split and Ike came over, shaking his head. "Do you believe that cat?" he asked.

Mr. Allen walked in with his usual air of urgency. "Anybody got a cigarette?" he asked. "Oh, hi, Mike. Did you hear we got our state money?"

I offered him a True Blue and said yes.

"Nobody got a Kool?" He took my True. "Excuse me, we got a staff meeting starting upstairs. You coming, Anna?"

They went upstairs. Ike greeted a new visitor.

"This place is getting to be a madhouse," Jesus said. "Hey, I bought me a little bug. Want to see it?" His Volks was parked in front, all clean and polished. "Now that I have transportation, I'm going to come down and see you again. You can help me with my writing."

When we came back we found Wally White pecking at the typewriter.

"Did you ask permission to use my machine?" Jesus asked him, half serious.

"Oh come on, man," Wally said. "Aren't we becoming the organization man? I was just waiting for you. I can't type anyway. You promised to type out this story for me."

"I haven't got time for that now. I still have to write up my morning counseling reports and there's a meeting starting upstairs."

"Oh, come on," Wally said. "You promised. Won't take but a minute anyway."

Jesus took the pages Wally handed him. Inserting a piece of paper in the machine, he asked, "What do you think I am, Wally, a typist?"

THREE CRISES IN THE LIVES OF DOPE FIENDS

by Wallace White

It was Sunday, the hardest hustling day in the week for dope fiends.

Me and suffering Sam was on the stroll looking for anything stealable. There wasn't anybody on the turf except toughie the cop. When Sam spotted him, he said: You know little man, all cops are kin to each other, they're all bastards. Just as Sam finished giving toughie his daily abuse we both noticed this broad getting out of a Cadillac.

There's our fix, I said.

We knew most women never lock car doors. This would be easy.

We walked over near the car, keeping an eye out for toughie, who had gone in the bar. I told suffering to stay on the point while I took care of business. First I searched the glove compartment, then I looked under the rugs. I had given up hope until I found this box on the car floor in the back. Just as I was getting out of the car Sam shouted: Watch out, here comes toughie.

Toughie must have spotted us the same time we spotted him, because we all started running at the same time. Me and Sam headed for the projects, running as fast as two sick dope fiends can when freedom is at stake. We heard toughie holler Stop, you bastards.

When we got to the second building I heard this shot. A second later I heard Sam holler, Little man I'm shot. I just kept moving, I knew I couldn't help him. As I ducked in the next building I heard another shot, but by then toughie was out of sight.

I came out of the projects on Lenox Avenue and headed for Bad Foot Nancy's house.

Blackie Blue Eyes let me in. The Professor and Flo the dog was taking off. I was winded, I had to catch my breath; then I remembered the box I was carrying for the first time. I noticed there was an envelope taped on the outside and my first thought was I had stole someone's present: I stopped trying to guess what it was and opened the envelope; there was a short note:

Brothers and sisters beware:
Never give your heart to a dog
To tear.

I unwrapped the box and turned it upside down on the bed. Everybody stopped what they were doing and just stared.

Ain't that a bitch: said Blackie Blue Eyes.

I be damn: said Flo the dog.

This is incredible: said the Professor.

Bad Foot Nancy looked at me in amazement: Little man you just stole a dead dog.

FIRE! FIRE!

It had snowed for three days and the weather had dropped to freezing. The streets were empty except for an occasional walker. Suddenly there appeared what at first seemed like three phantoms moving like race horses. As they drew near you could see it was a woman and two men. The three turned with one movement into the hallway of the large apartment house. On the third floor the woman put a key into the door of the room in the rear. They all seemed to be preparing for some great ritual. The woman brought a glass of water; the first man unwrapped a small package containing an eye dropper, a wine bottle cap and a hypodermic needle. The second man stepped forward with a grand flourish and a look on his face that said, "I am really the star of this show." Tossing cellophane bags on the table containing a white powder, the first man gently picked them up proceeding to open each with a razor blade; then he carefully emptied each into the wine top; he slowly measured water with the eye dropper, three equal portions, and lit some matches placing the heat under the wine top. As these preparations was going on, the woman was wrapping a tie around the upper part of her arm. All at once the second man looked at her as if she'd just materialized from thin air and said, "Nodding Marie, I don't know what the hell you are tying up your arm for, you went first this morning." Marie turned to him with tears running down her face and said, "Mad Daddy, I am sick, my bowers are about to break, please let me go first." The High Priest turned from the Altar as he said, "Look Mad Daddy and you too Nodding Marie, my name is Johnny One Nut, but before I let either one of you take off before me, I'll be Johnny No Nut. We all have been out there for five hours looking for this dope; there is a panic coming, tomorrow we may not find any more dope, so stop this bitching—somebody got to be last, and Nodding Marie you went first this morning go last tonight."

Nodding Marie began to name the trials and tribulations womanhood has suffered at the hands of a man. When Mad Daddy told her to shut up, this wasn't a woman suffrage meeting. When Johnny One Nut had finished taking off, he took off his wet sneakers. It was at that moment that Mad Daddy and Nodding Marie was sorry God had given them a nose. He passed the works to Mad Daddy; just as Mad Daddy finished shooting his dope there was a loud cry of fire, a great noise could be heard in the hall. Johnny One Nut cracked the door and peeked out; he could see people running to the fire escape at the end of the hall. Everybody was holding something in their hands and arms. One woman held her baby close to her and another woman was carrying a T.V. set; most men arms were filled with suits and shoes. There was cold fear in Nodding Marie's face as she picked the wine top up with the small amount of liqure in it; she followed Johnny One Nut, who was carrying his sneakers to the fire escape. As she moved down the stairs she said a prayer: "God don't let me drop this." Mad Daddy was moving fast and almost pushed Nodding Marie down the fire escape; she turned and informed him she had her fix in her hand and he should move down the fire escape in an orderly manner. When Marie touched the cold ground she gave God thanks for his mercy. A fireman in his haste to become a hero didn't see Marie and knocked the wine top with Marie's fix in it to the ground. Nodding Marie looked in disbelief as the hungry snow greedily ate her dope up. She turned to face the excited tenants with tears of disappointment and hopelessness in her face and screamed: "Who in the hell called the god damn fire department in the first place???"

THE POET LAUREATE OF DOPE FIENDS

I guess none of us really ever knew his name; all I remember is one day we looked up and there he was. At first we never paid much attention to him, but gradually we noticed he was always reciting some poem, so some one started calling him Shakesphere Jones. As time went by we would look for him after we had "copped" then we would all get high and listen to him run a poem down, something like "Honky Tonk Bud" or "The Fall", or "The Girl in the Blue Velvet Band." Sometimes someone wanted to hear something special, like "King Herion", this always meant that he would get a free fix. As time went by this was how he kept his habit up. Twice a day we would all meet: Miss Good Gash, "Flo the Dog," Blackie Blue Eyes, Suffering Sam, Lips, Bad Foot Nancy and Sticks. We would cop and go to Mack the Knife's house. After everybody had got off we would settle back and Shakesphere would get off on one of his poems. None of us ever heard one complete poem, just snatches. I remember parts of "The Fall"; that one always turned me on. Lets see if I can remember it, it went something like this; "She'll trick with Apaches, and Siouxs, Arabs and Jews, Greeks and Freaks and Breeds I can not even name." I would always come up out of my nod just as Shakesphere got to that part, and looking at him I could see his wild gestures and abnormally bright eyes, at this point I would always say, "Mr. Jones say that part again." Then everybody would come out of their nod selling wolf tickets, "Dig yourself lame." I would reply "Play dead chump." Amist the noise, dimly you could still hear Shakesphere, "She would trick in the house of God."

Addicts are creatures of habit, so you can imagine how everything was thrown off when one day Shakesphere couldn't be found. Flo the Dog had seen him earlier in the day; Suffering Sam had took off with him about one o'clock but no one had seen him since, as we stood around trying to figure out what had happened to Shakesphere, a police car drove up with an ambulance behind it; everybody's mind forgot Shakesphere for the moment to encounter this new mystery. Miss Good Gash had heard someone died of an O.D. on the roof of 57. As the attendant brought the body down, Suffering Sam slid up, we all turned to see who the new comer was. Sam stood with the sweat running down his face; Blackie Blue Eyes said, "Whats happening Suffering?" Sam just stood still for a minute as if he had stopped breathing, then slowly his mouth opened and the words just seemed to fall out. Without form or order, "Roof—Overdose—Dead—I tried—Shakesphere—Help him—. For a minute everything went motionless, there was no time, no breathing, no movement, just complete stillness. Slowly I could see Sticks lips move, but couldn't heard anything. Then I heard Lips say Damn!! Who's going to recite the poems now?

The End

Wally is short with a high-pitched voice and walks with a cane. "My mother was the black sheep in the family so I guess I'm the black sheep in this generation," he says. He was brought up by his uncle and aunt who both worked and were not exactly poor. Wally pronounces aunt, "ahnt."

"Let's say, perhaps I had a psychological hang-up. When I was in high school there was money being laid away for me to go on to college but I didn't stick to the program. I came from a predominantly female family and perhaps this was the fly in the ointment.

"My aunt in Jacksonville raised me but when I got to a certain age my mother came and wanted me. I didn't look upon her as a mother—I didn't know her that way, if you know what I mean. My aunt was my mother because she had raised me and taught me everything I knew. Rather than be with my mother, it seems that I would act up—now that I look back on it. I would run away from home, quit school—something. I just couldn't view her as my mother and this is where all my hang-ups came from. Me and her don't hit it off too tough.

"When she took me I started running away from home and getting into almost any kind of situation where I wouldn't have to be with her. I couldn't view her as my mother. When I got to the big city, I just had to survive on my own and so I automatically fell in with, you know, surviving types."

Wally is a graduate of ARC, in charge of statistics, and lives in an apartment a few blocks away. It was robbed four times this year; two television sets, two radios, one record player, his record collection, and most of his clothes were taken. He remembered all the times he'd done the same thing. As Malcolm X said, the chickens come home to roost. Wally believes in the balance of justice, in the inevitability of paying restitution.

He came out of the Navy with thirty-eight thousand dollars from shooting dice and playing poker and gave it to his mother who was going to get a business and a home and so forth, all of which never materialized. The money vanished. She burned him, you might say. It was the final wedge between them and he left home for good.

Wally was a second-story man for awhile—until he fell off a roof and crippled himself. That ended that career. Now he limps. He moved into forgery, busting into mailboxes for Welfare checks. After eighteen months he got caught at it and the FBI took all sorts of samples of his handwriting. So he had to find something else.

". . . I went into the begging field. One time I was standing in the subway and this lady comes up to me and hands me two dollars. And I says, wow—you know—like, wow! That's when I first thought seriously about it. I discovered that someone gets paid every day of the week in New York City. This is the theory I used—there are never any bad days. You just had to know the right places.

"It's very good money, in case you don't know it. Let's see, on a weekday I'd make anywhere from fifty-five to sixty dollars a day. Weekends would come to a little more—seventy-five or eighty. I went about it just like a job. I'd work from nine-thirty till about quarter to five, when the rush hour begins. Then the subway was too packed and I couldn't move from car to car.

"I'd go, cop my stuff, and be back by six-thirty to catch the theatre crowd. I'd work until eleven-thirty, sometimes twelve. I had it pretty good. It's a long day's work but you don't notice it when you got a habit.

"It's work, just like anything else. See, I had regular customers who gave me a certain amount every week. Every Friday night, there were a couple of people who would give me ten dollars at Wall Street. I could be sure of that, like clockwork.

"I found the best psychology is not to *say* anything, not to ruffle them up. Some people have an aversion to beggars. As long as you don't say nothin' they don't have an opening to vent their hostilities out on you. Maybe they are guilty about having a lot of money or something. Some people can always find a justification for not giving.

"That particular time, my habit was a three-year run. I hadn't gotten busted in three years—well, just overnight. The kind of hustling I was doing only called for, like, twenty days—and most of the time I could sob my way out of it. So I maintained my habit for three years, begging on subways."

Wally has read seriously since he was fourteen—since he

saw an ad in a magazine for a bargain deal on a package of books of all ages and types. He sent for them. He always maintained a little library, even in his addiction years. Lately he's been reading Negro history; Elijah Muhammed's *Black Man in America, The Autobiography of Malcolm X,* and *Crisis in Black and White.*

He writes at the rate of about a story a week. The best of them impressed me very much and, warning Wally it was a long shot, I took them down to Bob Brown, Fiction Editor at *Esquire.* I didn't really expect anything except some encouragement at best.

Esquire bought them. Calling Wally to tell him the news, I felt almost as elated as if they had accepted something of mine—not quite, but almost. So I was surprised and disappointed with his mild reaction: "Oh yeah. That's nice."

At his request, I made an appointment with Bob and went there to introduce them. After waiting half an hour, I figured Wally wasn't coming and left, too annoyed to call and find out why.

This sort of thing happens with ARC people. Allen is notorious for not returning calls and forgetting appointments. Jesus broke two dates. I volunteered to show Flagg through the Museum of Modern Art—Mrs. Kosof had assigned him a project on Picasso—but he blew our appointment and never called to explain either. Wally happened a week later and it was kind of the last straw.

But Wally did call, the same afternoon, to apologize. He had come fifteen minutes later and had had a good talk with Bob. "I got hung up in traffic," he explained.

Artistic temperaments ought to be allowed a certain leeway. And that should be the worst thing an inactive dope fiend is guilty of. I forgave him gladly.

The postscript to this chapter mirrors somewhat the end of the book. You've probably heard the joke: Q. "What do you call a Negro with a Ph.D. in psychology?" A. "Nigger."

Well, this is no joke. When he took his five-hundred-dollar *Esquire* check to the bank, the teller refused to cash it. An officer phoned Bob to verify the fact that it really belonged to this little, poorly dressed, crippled colored guy. Wally doesn't look like an *Esquire* writer.

From *New Life* (ARC newsletter):

MARTIN LUTHER KING, JR.

We, of Addicts Rehabilitation Center, although considered the most heartless, most cynical, most inconsiderate of human beings are filled with compassion, grief and sorrow. Martin Luther King, Jr. is dead. Our hearts are torn. When the mainstream of humanity grieved we grieved also. This issue of New Life is our humble attempt to express our feelings on the death of a Great Black Man.

13
I Want To Hold Your Hand

Wally, Bill Glenn, Mr. Allen, and I drove to Paterson, New Jersey, early one morning. Allen was to give a speech before a woman's group at a church over there and both he and Bill had been invited to attend a meeting of the Passaic County Board of Freeholders who were considering the problem of narcotics addiction in their community. Wally and I were just along for the ride.

The ladies were white, elderly, with newly beauty-parlored hair, rouged cheeks and wore little hats with plastic flowers. They brought cookies, cakes, and general goodies they had baked to serve at the coffee klatch after the morning festivities.

As they arrived, Wally and I were waiting by the auditorium door, Allen having gone back by the pulpit. Seeing me with him they apparently assumed I was in the program also, despite my lack of color. So they were extra kind greeting us.

"How do you do; my name is Mrs. Soandso. It's nice to have you boys with us this lovely morning."

"Boys!" I said to myself. Jeezus Christ, you should excuse the expression. One after the other like that, all so nice and considerate. Nice ladies whose husbands wouldn't think of hiring a black salesman, who give their old clothes to their maid who is always so appreciative; nice people who want civil, equal, and human rights for everybody but not at their expense or in their neighborhood.

They didn't seem to bother Wally one bit. He kept smiling

broadly and rapping in his pleasant tenor with all comers. "Yes, ma'am, that's right. I'm with the ARC program. Sure is nice to be here, ma'am."

My thoughts were about the hypocrisies and the endless trail of evil the church has left behind for well over a thousand years. Why, for instance, was this new building so opulent while there were still slums anywhere, let alone less than a mile away? All these nice ladies with their best clothes on, faces painted for the Lord; they didn't understand one goddam thing and I was in no mood to let them off the hook. Maybe Wally felt like Tomming them, but I didn't. Standing in a corner with shades on, unsmiling, I'm sure they thought I was not yet quite rehabilitated.

During a lull in the parade, I said, as ironically as possible, "You sure are pleasant this morning, Wally."

"Oh, these people don't know the difference," he said. "You can't blame them; they mean well. Did you know I'm anticipating joining the Manhattan Christian Reformed Church?"

"You are?" I was surprised, I don't know why. Many ARC people get religion either just before or after coming in. In terms of future soul sales, ARC is not all that bad an investment for Christian Reform Church, Inc. I see no reason to be grateful to them for spending their money on social services as long as my taxes are that much higher because they don't pay any. A child has no obligation to feel grateful to a father who keeps him on cornstarch while feeding himself steak.

"Why?" I asked.

"Well, when I was a kid, I never dug religion too tough. My father was a reverend; maybe that was the reason. You know? I always went out on my own—religion was something I could do without. It was something people talk about on Sunday and forget the rest of the week. Then . . . let's see . . . I guess it was back in the late fifties. I began re-evaluating the question.

"I got a taste of the Black Muslims. This kind of slanted my thinking for a while. As a matter of fact, I'm still receptive to a great many of the things they teach. But when it comes to the religious concept itself, they lose me. It doesn't make too much sense, not logically. And I'm the kind of person who, if he decides to support a thing, supports it wholeheartedly. But I must understand what I'm supporting, you know what I mean? Logically, they don't give me anything. I don't know if you are aware of the history of the twenty-four scientists and the oracles, but this is part of their doctrine and it really doesn't make too much sense to me, especially since I can't find any historical facts to support it.

"Actually, I feel as if I'm on the threshold of a religious awakening. I feel this. Sometimes I become confused, though, about whether I should accept Christianity as a black man's religion or whether it is really exclusively for white people. What kind of tipped the scales for me was the way the Manhattan Christian Reform Church operates. This is much different from other churches. You know, most churches are only concerned with their members. These people seem to be concerned with the whole neighborhood, member or otherwise, with human beings, in other words."

A lady with a red corsage and "official" ribbon came up to us and said gently, "If you gentlemen would like to go in now, the meeting is about to begin."

There was an invocation or whatever you call it, a prayer or two, a number of hymns sung by the wife of a minister in a not unpleasant contralto, some announcements about the whereabouts of former club members—one is now with her husband ministering to the natives in the heart of darkest

Uganda—the ancient ritual of plate passing and, finally, "our good friend Jimmy Allen" was introduced.

White people tend to call Mr. (Reverend) James Allen, "Jimmy." Curious. Ex-dope fiends call him "Mr. Allen." I call him "James," which even seems too informal. Not that he is up-tight or cold or anything—Allen can cat and mess around with the best of them. His relationship with the staff is quite loose, off duty. There is a lot of kidding.

Wally, particularly, takes every opportunity to put him on. For instance, the door to Allen's office locks automatically when it closes with the latch on. It won't open from either side without a key. Allen is always locking himself in, and a call must be made downstairs to Mr. Randolph or whoever has the house keys to come up and spring him. Allen has a lot of things to do, and is good and absentminded anyway, so it's easy to understand how a little thing like a latch can get away from him. Wally loves that. He sits at his desk in the adjoining office, smiling and saying, "I see Dodo's gone and done it again."

Wally writes a gossip column called "Dope on Ex-Dopeys" in the program's mimeographed publication, "New Life." You can always be sure of a juicy item about the chief:

> ". . . No one should feel bad when Mr. Allen asks someone why he looks funny. One night his wife, he and myself were watching TV and his wife dozed off and he jumped up and shouted, 'Mary, what's wrong with you?' . . . Mr. Allen kicked his smoking habit and got on everybody's nerves while doing so . . . J. Allen stays up all night studying out of his chess volumes and casually walks in and asks somebody to play and still loses. . . ."

However, it is always "*Mr.* Allen."

Not to the lady with the ribbon. "And now, without further

ado," she said into the microphone, "here is our friend, Reverend Jimmy Allen." She doesn't understand, it's not her fault.

Nor Allen's. He really laid it down, told it like it is. The problem of the addict and the ghetto is a white problem. It is no longer enough to say "I don't understand." It's your business to learn. Ignorance is no excuse, as any cop or judge will tell you. How can we talk about "unprecedented prosperity" when the plight of the black poor is what it is? How can we spend millions in Vietnam while our cities rot? He talked about the fire next time, pulling no punches. From the back where we were, Allen looked even smaller, everything but his head hidden behind a lectern and even half of that blotted out by a microphone. The truth generally looks small.

Afterwards, downstairs in the neon social hall, I sat at the table of honor with Wally and Allen flanked by ladies and a minister or two. Nice people, all of them. No smoking allowed. Oh, what marvelous cookies! You are writing a book? . . . Be sure and spell my name right . . . Hahaha. J-E-R-K.

It was over not a moment too soon. Thank you Mr. Allen, we all thought your talk was so informative. Allen's clip-on bow tie jiggled, he pushed his glasses up his nose, bowed just a bit as ministers do, thanked the thankers, smiled very politely and we bade our fond farewell.

Bill Glenn had been dropped at the Paterson City Hall to confer with some Christian Reform people who were bringing in a proposal for the establishment of a program modeled after ARC before the Freeholders. The meeting was in progress as we arrived.

Twelve Establishment types plus Bill and two others were sitting around a big table. Three were black, one Japanese, and all the rest looked Italian. A certain Mr. Berliner and the Japanese man were with the state and had come up from Trenton specially. They explained the law. There are no dollars in the New Jersey State budget for halfway houses, only after-care facilities on a day-care basis. The law, which had just been passed, states specifically, ". . . help will be provided for after-care. . . ."

Mr. Allen raised his hand politely. "May I say something?" They turned to him. "You realize of course . . ." the woman taking shorthand notes stopped. ". . . that after-care does not preclude residence facilities. Now, we have learned a long time ago that day-care just doesn't work. This is not a part-time job, helping the addict to reenter so-called normal society. Since the state of New Jersey is just beginning a program, it can benefit from ten years of experience those of us already in the field have had. One thing we have learned: day-care centers are not enough. It is impossible to play Ping Pong or checkers two hours a day and then go back out into the old environment every night; an addict will not be able to cope with normal responsibilities and pressures. We have learned that. Is there any way the law can be interpreted so as to set up at least a pilot halfway house program?"

No, there wasn't. You can't get there from here. The law says . . . you will make the same mistakes others have made before and the lousy junkies had better be grateful 'cause that's all they are going to get. (My interpretation.)

But, like the ladies in church, the Passaic Board of Freeholders are good people. They have been talking about this matter for three or four meetings now and, as one fat lady pointed out with a wheeze, it's better to get something going, even if it may not be the most ideal program, than to discuss it endlessly and do nothing.

The law under discussion required "professionals" in charge. The state would exercise close control and the bulk of the proceedings would be put in charge of "qualified" social workers and "trained" psychiatric personnel; just the ticket that had failed ninety-eight percent of the time in the past.

It turned out that the corpulent black man sitting across the table smoking a pipe, pushing hardest for a "professional" staff, was a "trained" psychiatrist and had offered his services at a discount—a sawbuck an hour. The pork barrel is alive and well in Passaic County.

But we should learn to put up with these things and, in the art of the possible, it is better for these good people to be concerned with solving the problem sloppily than not at all. Isn't it?

Allen made one more stab before adjournment, describing the growth of ARC to its present size—forty in-patients, five hundred day-care people—and relating the success he feels they have had with a setup run by ex-addicts, advised by professionals under them.

The animated discussion that followed revealed that there are presently no detoxification facilities in Passaic County and, indeed, the one place in the state of New Jersey an addict can clean up physically is in Trenton, where there are only sixty-four male and ten female beds.

One of the Christian Reform people, black, asked for the floor and got it. Obviously nervous, lighting a cigarette and stumbling for words, he pleaded that, whatever the Freeholders decide to do, "Let's not forget that we are dealing with human beings. This thing shouldn't be a political football, staffed with people who just want to get on a payroll."

Mr. Berliner got extremely up-tight with that and began defending himself loudly. He serves free, etcetera etcetera. How could anyone make such an accusation? "We are serious about this thing," he said.

Bill Glenn, who had been quiet and attentive throughout, now lost his cool. He shouted all the right things, many of which repeated what Allen had reasoned earlier. He accused the psychiatrist to his face. He berated the state of New Jersey for appropriating only a few hundred thousand dollars for such an important and difficult problem. He pointed out that New Jersey addicts that want treatment have to cross the river into New York which is hardly fair to New York taxpayers. He all but called them a bunch of phonies and finks.

Allen interceded and, diplomatic as always, quieted Bill down by pointing out that these people were trying to do all that was possible under the circumstances. They didn't make the law.

A motion was finally passed. A small, state-supervised day-care program would be set up, with the county matching state funds. In addition, a clinic would be opened—on the black psychiatrist's premises. He would be paid for that too. Politics, at least, are integrated in Passaic County.

The prolonged silence in the car driving back was finally broken by small talk. "How does it feel being a rich man, Wally?" Allen asked.

"What do you mean, rich?" Wally said. "I already lent out all the money from *Esquire*. Bread don't last too long around ARC—as a matter of fact you got some of it yourself." Wally smiled to show he really didn't mind.

"No, I mean . . . aren't you back on full salary this week?"

"What happened?" I asked.

"Oh," Wally said with a shrug, "let's put it this way. About two months ago I acted up a little bit; so I was demoted. I had been making eighty-six dollars a week and the chief cut me down to fifty-five. It just went back up."

"What did you do?"

"I just disappeared. I went away for about twelve days."

"Where did you go?"

"Well, I went to some friends up in Connecticut. I just

. . . I got to the point where dope fiends aggravated me, I couldn't stand being around them any more at that point."

"You didn't get on anything, did you?"

"No, no, no. This is the point. It got so I couldn't *stand* to look at dope fiends. They get on my nerves at times.

"After all, I've been involved with them for three years without a vacation, except for those twelve days. It just piled up on me, you know? It got to be too much of a mental strain, their laying all their troubles on me, telling me how much they need me an' all that. I'm too good a listener."

"Why didn't you just ask for a vacation?"

"Yeah." Wally looked over at Allen, driving, who showed no reaction. "I had been telling them this for a long time and they always say, 'All right, as soon as the grant comes through, as soon as we put on more staff, as soon as something else, blah, blah, blah.'

"You see, I used to be house manager before Randy. That job is kind of like being a policeman, mother, father, lover, and everything else. We had about ten guys then and only one house manager, which was me. And, as you know, this is a twenty-four hour thing. I didn't have any time for myself. Then they changed me to another position, which was cook, and that was just about as bad as being house manager because everybody was always hanging out in the kitchen and they still used me to bounce things off of. They'd always be running something down to me.

"This is one of the reasons I'm in statistics. It's away from all that. For some reason it seems that I have the type of personality that makes people want to tell me deep dark secrets they been holding in for years. This is a fault of mine; other people say it's not a fault, but I think it is. What am I going to do with all those problems?

"I wouldn't even mind if it was just a matter of somebody getting it off his chest—I wouldn't mind that. But when they are finished telling me their stories, they always ask, like, 'What should I do?' He's taking it off himself and putting it on me. . . . Strange as it may sound, though, even though I do get mentally aggravated sometimes, I really do enjoy the work."

We were approaching the tollbooths at the George Washington Bridge by then. Taking the money out of his pocket, Allen said, "I hope there's a pretty girl at the booth. Whenever there's a pretty girl there, I always make it a point to hold her hand and see what she does."

The girl turned out to be an older woman so Allen just handed over the fifty cents. He did sing her a little snatch of a song however; "I want to hold your hand. . . ."

"I just don't understand those people," Bill said, still thinking about the Freeholders. "Don't they ever learn anything? Don't they see what they are doing? While they go through their meetings and shenanigans, people are out there suffering and dying. Those people need help, can't they see that? I just don't understand."

"I never seem to get a pretty girl at them tollbooths," Allen said. "Seems like I don't have no kind of luck. . . . Bill, forget about it. There's no sense aggravating yourself; nothing you can do about it anyway. They'll just have to find out for themselves."

14
Shame on You

One Saturday afternoon, just as the Packers/Rams game was beginning on television, the phone rang. My friend Bruno calling. He is driving his girl Robin to New Haven for a concert by a rock group called the Doors. He is a photographer, she a writer, and they are working on a story for *Life*. Did I want to come along? I decided the Doors were more interesting than the Packers.

When we stopped just over the Connecticut border for gas and coffee, a patrol car pulled in with roof-light flashing. A touch of panic . . . but the trooper was only interested in Bruno's Arizona license plates.

Anybody who has carried pot will understand. Routine brushes with the police are each a potential disaster. No matter how cool you look or act, what is in your pocket puts you in jeopardy. All cops are enemies. While this one checked Bruno out, I remembered a similar roust.

Five of us were in a station wagon on the Indiana Turnpike. Just before dawn, a siren sounded behind us—and that same rotating light. It was foggy and cold so the windows were closed. The smell of pot was strong. Max, driving, threw out his lit joint and we tried to air the car out before pulling over.

"Oh shit," Max said. "This is it. Wait till he sees all those instruments in the back." Cops suspect all musicians in this country. And we didn't look too cool anyway. We had worked earlier in the evening, were hollow-eyed, needed shaves, and didn't look particularly "normal" to begin with. If this cop gets curious, if he is alert and good at his job, we are sure to be busted. God knows what's on the floor or behind the seats after three weeks of one-nighters.

The trooper leaned in the window. "You were doing ninety back there; you realize that, Buddy?" His cracker twang wasn't very encouraging. "Let me see your license."

Max was cool. He smiled, relaxed and friendly—even innocent. "No. Really? I didn't know it was that fast. Sorry. There weren't any cars on the road and I guess I just wasn't watching the speedometer."

Shining a flashlight inside, the trooper saw the horns. I could see the morning headlines—BANDMEN ARRESTED ON DOPE RAP. "You guys musicians?" he asked.

"That's right, officer. We're playing a dance in Splodunk tonight."

"What band are you with?"

"Sonny Barry."

"Oh, really? I remember him when he was featured with Kent Standish. Sonny's some trumpet player. Can he still hit those high notes? I used to play a little trumpet myself in high school. What do you guys play?"

Max told him he was a drummer and we all introduced ourselves. The trooper was now downright friendly, happy to have met some celebrities. Finally, he wrote out a warning and said to be more careful in the future.

The cops in New Haven weren't going to be so loose.

Before the concert, Bruno, Robin, and I went for a pizza. The guy with no sideburns and a flat-top who served us looked like Dean Rusk's idea of the "enslaved" people behind the iron curtain; pasty, unsmiling, without spirit. A Coke clock and Coke posters decorated fresh walls. A plant near the door had a ribbon on it: "Congratulations." A fat family, out for a big Saturday-night treat, ate without looking at or talking to each other. The kid kept dripping spaghetti sauce on his pants. Here was too much reality; some hick's free-enterprise dream come true. A business of his very own. A cleanclean, neon and Formica business founded on new-world principles and artificial seasoning. The pizza was lousy.

We walked to the concert a few blocks away, through a neighborhood of gas stations, hardware stores, bars, laundromats, and brick taxpayers. Plenty of cops around. Cops with baggy pants and unshined shoes. Cops walking to work in pairs swinging billy clubs. Dumb-looking old cops. Burly cops with red faces, only a few young cops with some humanity remaining. All cops ready to defend the Republic against obscenity and hair.

The New Haven Arena is a run-down hockey rink. We had "ice seats," second row front-and-center. The place was filled with teenyboppers and Yalies—few townies, not many hippies, and quite a few cops. About two thousand people in all. It was cold and drab like the neighborhood—and like the first group, locals named "Tommy and the Rivieras"; two saxophones, guitars, organ, and drums thumping and clanging while three girls fresh from the beauty parlor in spangled mini-dresses sang unheard into a dead microphone. Then we listened to the "Lochsley Hall Assembly," a second local group. I missed the Packers.

After the intermission, three Doors came through the curtain dressed flower-casual; plugged-in, tuned-up, and relaxed. Then, Jim Morrison and many teenybopper screams. Such a lovely neck he has, all framed in hair. An erection was obvious through his tight vinyl pants. He is chief Door and the first American male sex symbol since James Dean, so they say.

More cops around the stage now; serious and bitter.

Morrison started freaking out his act; grinding, bumping, and coming close to sucking the microphone. If you had a dirty mind, you might call it obscene. His eyes were oh-so red. If I were a cop I'd arrest him for just looking that way.

Two teenyboppers flitted down front and flashed their Instamatics. More of them. They sat, looking up at their funky hero with rapture.

Unhappy girl, fly fast away,
don't miss your chance to
swim in mystery.

Morrison rolled the heavy round microphone base with his feet as he sang, holding the pole with one hand, barely under control.

People are strange
When you're a stranger.

He separated the mike from the base and heaved it off the stage, missing the kids sitting down front by not that much. The cops moved out. Somebody's daughter sitting in the aisle next to me was dragged by her scruff, the cop copping a little feel in the process. The other little girls went back to their seats under similar pressure.

Things settled down, but the police were staring up at Morrison with undisguised hate as he went into a soliloquy, the rhythm section vamping quietly behind him.

"I want to tell you a story. It happened to me very recently, just a few minutes ago, right here in New Haven, Connecticut." He continued, slow, deliberate, almost poetic. ". . . Yes. That's right . . . right here in New Haven . . . Connecticut. My friends here (waves to the band) and I went out for . . . a sandwich and a drink just before . . . the concert . . . got to talking with the waitress there . . . she asked for our autographs . . . said it was for her daughter . . . but I knew she wanted it for herself . . . came back here

. . . right here in New Haven, Connecticut . . . this girl and I went in the shower room to . . . get acquainted . . . to get to know each other. This is a true story . . . it happened right here in New Haven, Connecticut . . . just a few minutes ago. . . . A little man in blue comes in and says [with an Amos-and-Andy accent], 'Watchoo doin' heah? Break it awuph. Move awon' . . . There's no love in the world . . . sometimes I feel so alone . . . like nobody loves me. . . ."

A teenybopper ran down the aisle, her face falling apart. "*I* love you," she screamed. "I LOVE YOU!" The cops were huddled on each side of the stage like a football team going over the game plan.

". . . So, this little man in blue . . . he takes out a shaving can . . . and, right here in New Haven, Connecticut . . . only a few minutes ago . . . he squirts it in my face . . . and I'm blind . . . he blinds me . . . I was blind for five minutes . . and now they are red and they itch."

". . . Yes, ladies and gentlemen . . ." Hard rock time began together, as if this routine was routine. Morrison leaned back, the bulge in his pants bulging even more. "WE WANT THE WHOLE FUCKING WORLD AND WE WANT IT . . . NooOOwwWW!"

That did it. Two police platoons moved out. Morrison bowed to spotty applause. The lights came on. The Door on organ whispered in Morrison's ear—something like "Let's get out of here," I guessed. Ignoring him, Morrison shouted, "Do you want to hear one more?"

"Oh yes. Yes. Yeaaayy." A clump of teenyboppers chanted, "YESYESYESYES." Most people were leaving. We were standing. Morrison was salty, extremely salty—on some kind of verge. "Okay, then turn the lights out. We're not finished yet. Turn out the lights . . . LIGHTS. LIGHTS." He stood stiff, defiant, waiting for a response.

Then so-called reality came to the New Haven Arena. (That's the way it is, the way it really is.) The curtains behind the stage parted for Lieutenant Kelly in braid, Irish grey hair neat around his officer's cap—a poster cop. He posed for fully a minute, hands on hips. It was a catharsis, a sniff of immortality, a flash of clarity. Here was the essence of America. Now! The Establishment against youth. Law versus individual expression. The police against everybody. The definitive bust. A Godard freeze. H-O-L-D . . . I-T. . . . . . .

Chaos. Girls hysterically crying as more cops poured on stage. They wrestled with Morrison, finally hustling him off. The loudspeaker started a march. "Be kind to our web-footed friends, for a duck may be somebody's mo-ther. . . ." No announcement. No explanation. No psychology. No police science. Not much discipline. Just a lot of pushing. "Okay, okay. Move on. Everybody out. It's all over folks. Let's go. MOVE."

Five cops converged on a kid in the lobby. Bruno took pictures. When one of the cops saw him, he charged over and kneed him in the back, throwing him out through the door into the street, despite his prominent red "working press" card. Bruno went up to Lieutenant Kelly, who saw it all, showed him his press card, and requested an apology, "as a matter of courtesy." Kelly was very polite and said, "Very well, I'll take care of that in a minute, sir."

Shortly thereafter, Bruno saw the cop who had hit him and demanded the apology. The cop said, "You want trouble? Arrest this man." He twisted Bruno's arm behind his back, hustled him to the squad car and roughly frisked him, squeezing his balls several times. Bruno kept saying, "Okay, okay. I'm going quietly. I'm not armed." He mentioned that he was English and that he had spent two years with the press in Vietnam.

Robin saw Bruno's arrest and, approaching the officer, said

"Patrolman, you have a member of the press and I suggest you release him." She tugged at his sleeve and asked for Bruno's cameras. The cop said, "You want to get arrested, too? Grab that woman."

Maybe it was nervousness. His face twitched and his hand shook. The word "orgasm" crossed my mind.

Robin was put in a squad car with Bruno. I approached the car and said, "Excuse me, officer, but I'm with these people. Can you tell me . . . ?" He shouted, "He's one of them—you're under arrest too."

See what I mean? Never talk to cops.

We were booked into a Saturday night tank, well stocked with drunks yelling for cigarettes, water and moaning. They took our belts. (Robin had been dropped off at the ladies' pen.) Bail was set at three hundred dollars each. Morrison, a few cells down, was not much of a sex symbol, slumped on a bench, his eyes still red and teary from the MACE which had been sprayed at him.

Our cell, like his, was a dirty cubicle furnished with only a splintery wooden bench and a toilet with neither seat nor flusher. It stank. The steel wall was covered with graffitti: "Drunk, March 2nd." "Pee Wee, 1961," and other such historical data. Doors clanged for hours as we were ignored, without water, cigarettes, or the opportunity to make a phone call.

Around five thirty, another drunk was locked up next door. He sang a soggy song. "OOooh, you're breaking my heart . . . shame on you . . . OOooh, shame on you. . . ."

15
Another Day Has Went in This World

It was reported by the media—"Seize Singer & Three at Rock Concert," said the *Daily News*. My image improved considerably up at the Center.

One thing learned early in the street: never tell the truth to Whitey, particularly if he's a "square." I'm both, although having played jazz brings me closer. You'd be surprised at all the guys in Harlem who were "just like that" with Charlie Parker, or "really tight" with Miles Davis. Jazz musicians were drop-outs before the term was coined, smoked grass before it was fashionable, were beat before beatniks, hip before hippies, and invisible along with the Invisible Man. To that extent every jazz musician—who earns the name—is a black man. I inherit some pigment from that. Being busted is even better. That's status in Harlem.

Even Garwood X smiled at me. Lindy Stokes was obviously knocked out. Flagg gave me some skin. Mrs. T. paid me the supreme compliment: "Mr. Mike is soulful," she said.

Mrs. T. is very worried about her daughter, who had been picked up for narcotics the night before. It is very hard to know how to react when you are told something like that. "Oh dear, I *am* sorry," seems inadequate; "Good God! Are you kidding?" much too square. I shook my head somewhere in between.

"Mr. Mike, I've been off narcotics over five years now. But, what with my daughter's troubles and all, I started to get that old urge again lately. I figured I'd better come around for some support. Know what I mean?" For some reason she laughed.

Mrs. T. is burned white on her arms, side, and part of her face. She had lipstick on and her hair was pulled back with some care. As usual she wore stockings rolled up to her knees. Her enormous thighs prevent her from closing her legs demurely enough to hide them. She laughs easily, all the time, and her breasts shake like family-size portions of jello.

"Mr. Mike, look at today's paper."

The New York *Daily News,* forever in search of pop poetry, carried a headline on page three: "He Was a Dope on Drugs; Now He's Hope to Others." Underneath were pictures of Mitch Rosenthal and Candy Latson, the latter having been newly appointed—along with eleven other Synanon graduates, calling themselves the "Dirty Dozen"—to a top post in Dr. Ramirez's City Narcotics Coordinator's Office.

"This is good publicity for the Center," Mrs. T. concluded. "There seems to be more hope for addicts now, Mr. Mike. Years ago, people didn't care at all about helping us."

She blinked like a good-natured, rather lovely frog, and pointed to her burns. "I fell asleep one night in a hotel downtown, on Sixth Avenue. Three weeks later I woke up in the hospital with these. There was a sort of makeshift tent over me because the sheet would stick to where the burns was. Soon's I woke up, the nurse called in this young intern. 'You're alive!' he said first thing. 'Now don't worry—as hard as you fought till now, we're goin' to be sure and take very good care of you.'

"I was in the hospital for months and months and when I was well enough to leave, I went right over to Welfare, down on twenty-eighth and Park, to have them reopen my case. My regular worker was out that day and the lady taking her place wanted to put me in a roomin' house on a hundred and fifteenth street.

"I knew that was a dope house and I told her uh-uh—no. She said there was no other place available. I said I'd go to the women's house of detention and come back the next day and talk to the lady who normally handles my case. She finally found me another place, on the same street but down the block, on the other side.

"They usually give you cab fare but, you know, Mr. Mike, that woman told me to take the subway—weak as I was—take the train to Grand Central, transfer to the shuttle, and then walk to the uptown train. All that walkin' and me with my suitcase and just out of the hospital . . . I just know that lady put the cab fare in her own pocket. Some people!"

Mrs. T. means white people, of course, but I'm not quite soulful enough for her to lay that bit of nitty on. Never will be, either, no matter how many nights I spend in jail.

Conversation is raucous before lunch and there is a lot of clowning in the basement dining room, which is cheerfully painted and not much like a basement. The long, wooden table is covered with clean plastic and piled high with white bread, bowls of spaghetti, greens, and various hot sauces.

"Okay . . . okay, everybody quiet down if you want to eat," Mr. Randolph says. "Let's have one minute of silence."

Hang your head for a while until, without consulting his watch, Randy signals the end. Platters of southern fried chicken appear and everybody digs in.

"Hey Mike, have you read this?" Wally shouts from across the table. He holds up a copy of Freud's speeches in America. "I was waiting for a guy yesterday and went into a bookstore to kill time. . . ."

". . . Pass the rabbit food, will you?" Randy asks, and I give him a bowl of collard greens. "You've been doin' a lot of research, Mike. What do you think of the methadone program?" It is the first time Randy has spoken to me, let alone asked for my opinion.

"I don't much care for the idea."

"Me either. Mike, I've known so many guys on that stuff and they just stay out of their heads all the time. A lot of them save up their tablets for a day or two and take them all at once to get really high. The way they nod out, I can't see any difference from heroin." (He pronounces it heroyn.)

Methadone is a synthetic drug which blocks heroin. It's legal if you join one of the programs set up around the country to distribute it. It is easy to take, and cheap; pennies a dose. Methadone is habit-forming, although non-escalating. Except for Mrs. Marie Nyswander and the others involved with methadone maintenance programs, this drug is held in general disrepute around rehabilitation circles. Theoretically, there is a therapy program which supplements the dosage, but it is modest and run by professionals, not ex-addicts, and ex-addicts seem to be the only ones who have any success getting dope fiends off stuff. Methadone keeps you sedated, forever high. Since you don't have to steal or mug to get it, society is satisfied. In other words, it's okay to stay sick, just don't bother us.

"They look just like they had a couple of good jolts of stuff," Randy is adamant. "The way it strikes me, all they are doing is substituting the dispensary for their connection. I don't see the point in that. Do you, Mike?"

"No. It's like saying, 'We have discovered two things: a simple substance which will arrest cancer, and a more complicated, lengthy process which will probably cure it. You are not worth the trouble or expense of the cure, so we will leave you hanging the way you are.' "

"It's like the plague, the Bubonic Plague," somebody says on the other end.

Luncheon conversation remains hectic, fragmented, and loud; mostly about dope. Rocky and two or three of the newer residents do not participate except to request platters passed to them.

One gets one's own coffee from an urn on the kitchen counter, at one end of the room. "I think I have a caffeine habit," Garwood says to me in the line.

"All these years, I've been prayin' for a miracle because I figured only a miracle could get me off drugs. And it occurred to me that I got my miracle—our miracle. I find out now that I am grateful for a thing called LSD. L-S-D, man. . . ."

Bill Glenn looks at Lindy Stokes who looks at Mrs. Boatright who looks at Mrs. Kosof who looks puzzled.

Pancho smiles. ". . . I'll explain what I mean. We know that Wall Street is where all the money goes. And I've got sense enough to know—because I've been in the business world—that wherever there's money there's some kind of power. And drugs make a bunch of money so there has to be a *lot* of people in so-called respectable society corrupted by this money. You understand?

"Now, the problem has been here all along, brother, but now the power structure is beginnin' to pay attention to it. Why? LSD is a drug that started functionin' not in the slums but in the suburbs, in the universities. All kinds of big people started talkin': 'Hey, keep it quiet but my son is usin' drugs.' Now these people are sayin', 'What are we goin' to do?'

"Money, man, money. 'We better spend some money to solve this problem.' Power is worried. The problem's here all the time, right? But now they gettin' concerned because it's too close to home. All the time, all you ever heard from those people was about drug addicts stealin' and murderin'; drug addict this and drug addict that. All bad. Now, all of a sudden, you hear somethin' good about drug addicts. They talkin' that rehabilitation talk now. They call their congressman and say, 'You better put some money in there!' We been here all these years, you see, but all of a sudden they concerned, really concerned. And somethin's happenin'. They're concerned, man. They're *concerned.* So, I see all this and I say yeah. YEAH! LSD."

Mrs. T. looks at me and nods her head knowingly.

"What about the police?" Bill asks the group. "Do you think the police are any more enlightened? Are they too becoming concerned about addicts?"

"No, definitely not," Lindy says. "I think they still give out a lot more static in impoverished neighborhoods. Not just Harlem, you know. I think you get a better play down in The Village because if they bust somebody down there, they don't know who they got. Might be a multi-millionaire's kid or something."

"I thought everybody was free and equal in this country." I am quite bitter after New Haven.

The laughter is heavy. Lindy says, "If you got little dollars, you a little free; you got big bucks you big free. And if your money is bigger than that, you don't have to worry about the police force at all. Did you read somethin' about the flower party that they had in Tompkins Square? All them kids smokin' pot—they called it a smoke-in or somethin'. Nobody got busted, right? But if we all went over and got high in Morningside Park, if we rolled up some tea and smoked it, we would all get busted. That's the difference right there.

"I think they ought to have more psychiatrists checkin' and analyzin' these people before they become policemen because some of them have sadistic tendencies. They might have an inferiority complex or somethin' and a lot of them don't seem to like kinky hair, solid colors, straight hats, lame people, blind people—or some combination. They should be checked-out better; they got so much power."

"Who's going to check out the people checking them out?"

"Mr. Zwerin seems to be a bit caustic this afternoon," Bill Glenn says. "Would you like to tell us about it?"

I tell about the bust in detail. Everybody listens politely, tolerant though not particularly impressed.

"Man, so now you see. When somethin' happens to you then you understand what we live with all our lives."

"It's very hard for us to have a respect for the law when that sort of thing goes on all the time."

"Wouldn't nobody call a cop for help in Harlem. They just mean trouble. Stay out of their way, that's what I always try to do."

The responses don't help my cool. "But somebody's got to do something about it. We can't just sit by with our heads in the sand all the time."

"You gotta remember it's different if you have a sheet—and I got a sheet this long. They can really sock it to you when you've got a sheet," Lindy says.

The guys go on to tell stories of injustices heaped on them by the law. No doubt many are exaggerated, some even invented. Remember, you cannot trust a junkie; they will con and lie and make you pity them as naturally as they breathe. These habits linger on long after detoxification. The stories are, however, quite plausible.

"I'm sick and tired of going to bat for some Joe Sploe," a voice floated upstairs.

I was alone in my room for the night, worried about the possibility of rats. It was in the unfinished wing of the Center's double brownstone and contained only three iron cots with old mattresses on them, all lumpy. The walls were snot-green and peeling. The only light in the room came from the street. There were no window shades. Small gnats flew around, harmless enough but bred in garbage it seemed to me.

Through the window I could see a bent, elderly woman pressing clothes in Bea's Laundry, even though it was after eleven, helped by a small boy. I wondered if there were rats over there. Everybody has heard about the rats in Harlem, we have seen the pictures of children with holes in their faces, we are used to saying, "Oh isn't that terrible." But being right there, knowing they aren't very far away, is something else. I started with every creak, rustle, and scratch.

". . . Man, I don't care what time it is. There's a man noddin' out in the house and it's your job to talk to him." It sounded like Lindy Stokes downstairs.

"Look, I've already informed Mr. Allen and . . ." (that was probably Randy) ". . . he said he'd take care of it first thing tomorrow morning. Now there's no sense making a big hassle about it in the middle of the night and disturbin' everybody else."

"How in the world do you expect me to go to sleep worryin' about some dope fiend fallin' asleep in bed holdin' a cigarette and burnin' down the entire joint?" Who could they be talking about? "Come on up with me anyway and talk to him."

They faded away and new voices appeared.

"You goin' out? Sign the book."

"Not me. I'm on restriction."

"You? You're not on restriction."

"I'm not? If I'm not, Jack, I wish someone would tell me about it. . . ."

". . . Mr. Truman don't look so good. He's got bags under his eyes. Somethin' wrong with you, Mr. Truman . . . ?"

I could hear Aretha Franklin from a distance. Some doors slammed. A toilet flushed. The lady and the boy closed up Bea's. A couple of drunks weaved down the middle of the street, passing their jug. My Pan American bag fell from the next mattress to the floor. Poor balance or rats?

More voices, a little laughter and some lazy yawns from

downstairs. ". . . Well—another day. Another day has went in this world. . . ."

Breakfast is fried eggs, bacon, white bread, and strong coffee: good grease. The day is one of those New York specials when the entire city smells like one big fart. The weather bureau calls it "haze." "The air is always worse in Harlem," Wally says. "It has something to do with the air currents." He is quite serious about it and who am I to argue?

"We have a crisis on our hands." Mr. Allen is furious. "All sorts of rumors are spreading around town that we have the lousiest program in New York City, that I'm letting all sorts of people in here high. Do you all know that we have a guy kicking his habit cold turkey in the house? Do you know that, Mr. Flagg?"

According to Mr. Allen, the Program is continually threatened. Somebody downtown always wants to close it up. It's a good way to keep the guys in line, but his independent—even defiant—attitude towards the politics of the rehabilitation game hasn't exactly made him friends or influenced influential people.

As a matter of fact, all programs have problems but, being more public-relations conscious, most of them hide their failures under a mass of misleading or irrelevant statistics. Allen is honest enough to talk about his failures, to not sweep his splitees under the carpet. He was completely open with me. I have had complete run of his place. There were no setups, no window displays of clean junkies for my benefit. I have been able to speak to anybody, any time, anywhere.

Flagg smiles with utmost innocence. "It's only a toothache, Mr. Allen—honest." If he could just take three or four aspirin and lie down in the day room, he'd be okay in a little while.

"Yes, you better do that, Mr. Flagg. Lindy, stay with him."

It is like in school: the teacher has just caught someone cheating. Have others been doing it? Does he know about them? Will he keep everybody after school? The meeting is subdued; most people look at the floor.

"Mr. Flagg is trying his best to get kicked out, so he doesn't have to make the decision himself. I think we should oblige him. He's not ready for rehabilitation and I think we'd better recognize it. It's a shame with a man who has been here as long as he has, and believe me, nobody feels worse about it than I do, but I think he'd better leave before he contaminates others."

Mr. Randolph takes Nix to pack Flagg's bags. They bring them down and escort him through the meeting area and out the door. Still holding his cheek as if with a toothache, Flagg puts on shades. Nobody says goodbye.

The meeting goes on to take care of business, although it is obvious that nobody's heart is really in it. Why did B.B. spend all his money last week; what could he have spent it on? There is a lecture on budgeting. Stop making all that noise upstairs; the neighbors will complain. Who didn't take the garbage out last night? The room is terribly overheated, my ass is numb, my eyes heavy. Mr. McCarthy has had a very negative attitude lately. These meetings are not the easiest part of the rehabilitation process. Allen should juice them up, or cut them down. Two hours to go. My mind wanders. I remember a party. . . .

I was invited for cocktails at a large apartment in the Dakota, a society affair for a charity concerned with addiction. The guest of honor was Dr. Efram Ramirez, the 38-year-old head of the New York City Addiction Services Agency, a part of the Human Resources Administration.

If that sounds bureaucratic, it is. And since Dr. Ramirez seems loose, even hip, I hit him right away with, "Do you really expect to accomplish anything from within the Establishment?"

"Yes—of course." He spoke for the record. He knew who I was— "When I made a decision to become involved seriously—professionally and personally—with the problem of rehabilitation, I became very rapidly aware that it required a basic change in the social system.

"You can deal with social systems in one of four ways. You can conform—I'm not a conformist. You can create a separate system like Synanon or the hippies—I don't believe in creating islands because I come from one. You can burn it down through armed revolution—I'm a pacifist. Or you can change it from within, through peaceful means. That's what I'm doing. I am an overt under-cover agent of change. I speak freely of upsetting traditions, I do not try to hide my feelings on the subject.

"Let me give you one example. When we are talking to the addict in the street, trying to motivate him to rehabilitate, we make it very clear that we are not offering him adjustment to the standard accepted system. We are offering him membership in a social revolution. We are not interested in making him a 'square.' 'Square' is to work from nine to five in a job which you don't particularly like, in a living lie, stifling your own creativity and just following the trend, accepting the outward status requirements of society—and then blowing up at five o'clock with four martinis.

"Who wants to live like that? Not me. I don't want to be a square, so I have no right to ask an addict to be a square either. I want to be productive, to have my own personal set of values. So I say to the addict: 'If you come in here just to dry out and to make believe you are back in society in an acceptable form while you are stifling your own creativity, I don't want to have anything to do with you . . . that's why I think methadone is a fraud.

"Let's talk about goals; if we talk about rehabilitation as a process, what are the goals of that process? Methadone is a fraud because it does not lead in any way towards the social revolution I am concerned with. It is a very materialistic concept. 'We don't care what happens to you; just don't steal from me.' That's why the goddam thing is so popular. Because it strikes a chord, you know. It is a simple solution, people think, to a complex problem; very attractive. The problem is much deeper than that. It's throughout every neighborhood. I say 'neighborhood,' not 'community.' When people talk about 'communities,' they talk about an image they have. Because Harlem is not a community. I don't know of any single area in New York City which *is* a community, with a community of interests and concerns and mutual help.

"So community is a goal we have, an ideal. We want to turn neighborhoods into communities the same way that we turn an addict into a productive, self-sufficient, creative individual. We want to turn neighborhoods into productive, realistic communities. Rehabilitation is the beginning—what most people consider the end of their work is the beginning for us.

"Staying away from drugs is just learning to walk. It's a minor thing. Ninety-nine percent of the total population of the world stays away from junk. Big deal. The question is, *now,* what are you going to do with your life?

"I chose to do this kind of thing with addicts because these are the individuals in our society who are under most pressure to do something about their alienation. Most people are under some form of alienation but very few of them feel any pressure to give it up. But addicts, delinquents, psychopaths, alcoholics: they are under a tremendous amount of pressure.

"They're at the end of their line. Society expects them to move somehow. They are the worst possible testing ground—with only one advantage: the pressure.

"We get criticized from all sides. The medical profession criticizes this whole idea of using ex-addicts but they go along with it now, reluctantly, because it's a fad. They go along with it for the wrong reasons. Basically they resent it, resent it profoundly. And it's not just intellectual resentment. The way that most professionals in the helping professions have shown this resentment is to become paternalistic and condescending. Of course I want my patient to come up, become a member of *my* team—as an aid, as Establishment ex-patient, a 'boy.' Out of the six large components of my program, four right now are being directed by ex-addicts, ex-addicts who have psychiatrists working for them. That bothers a lot of people—because I have inverted the structure."

. . . How do you do, Mrs. Mellon. This is such a *lovely* party. Yes, isn't Dr. Ramirez just divine? . . .

The taxi driver who picks me up on the corner asks, "Are you coming from the precinct?"

"No," I am quick to deny. I explain about ARC.

"Yes, drugs are getting to be a very serious problem." He is an elderly black man with a fine face. The *New York Times* is next to him on the seat. "I had a strange experience just last week. I was waiting for a light on Broadway and seventy-fourth and this young white girl comes over to my cab. She wasn't bad looking either. She says, 'Mister, I need a dollar bad. One more dollar and I can get a fix. Mister, I'll do anything you want if you'll give me a dollar: anything.' Imagine! Anything; for one dollar."

"What did you do?"

"Poor kid, I just gave her a dollar."

16
One of Them

Horny courts grind away, day after day, while you and I—you anyway—go oblivious about everyday business out in so-called normal society.

Drunks with scabby faces named McCabe, Jones, Kelly, and Christopher weave their way to the bench:

"Ten days, suspend execution."

"Five days, sentence suspended."

"You've had nine straight suspended sentences . . . ten days!"

Lock him up. Who cares?

Then there are the breakers, the enterers, the armed robbers, car thieves, the disturbers of our peace, alimony welchers. Relatives, friends, witnesses, and accused sit quietly, resigned in the chock gallery—blank, submissive, terribly sad, and mostly black. What does the law do for these people?

The court will come to boredom. Boredom please, boredom in the court. The sixth circuit court of New Haven is now in session. We are charged: breach of the peace, resisting arrest, and interfering with police officer Grandly in the execution of his duties.

Grandly had been right of course. I am indeed one of "them." His instincts are sound. A guy like me must be guilty of *something*.

You should know patrolman Grandly, badge number 999; his cherubic, dimpled cheeks, his Kraut crew cut. His eyes are a hundred percent cop; cold, dull, shifty. He is a puree in uniform and I suggest you stay out of his way.

Life had hired a member of the Connecticut bar to defend Robin, Bruno, and me. I was paying my own third and worried about it.

The New Haven courthouse is a thing out of Dickens; a Victorian monstrosity, patched, peeling, dimly lit, and smelly. An empty pint of Bon-Core port wine—"Pure California, alcohol 20% by volume"—stands by the door. Crooked, dirty shades cover dirtier windows. Sixty-foot ceilings support forty-foot unpainted chains on the end of which are neon strips. Paint peels around the clock, which is slow. Only the slowly turning ceiling fans are missing.

On the other side of the barrier: the boys. The courthouse gang. Bailiffs, clerks, bondsmen, stenographers, assistant D.A.s, cops, detectives; you know them—the guys. Jack Ruby was like that. They took the little woman out for pizza last night. Their conversation is dirty jokes and bowling scores. Waiting for their scene to get going. And clearly it is theirs. You are uncomfortable, they are not. You don't know correct procedure, they do. You have no idea how long you will have to wait, they don't care—the courthouse in-crowd.

"Everybody stand!" Justice creaks to the bench, a very old and not so wise-looking man with an extremely sour, red face. Thank God we only had to plead not guilty.

A week later Jim Morrison paid the city of New Haven $1,500 for having violated his constitutional rights. The deal: "Tell ya what, fella—you drop da bail and we just forget about da whole ting. Dat way everybody saves a lotta trouble. Okay?"

The flower people in L. A. said okay, a practical decision. Think of all those lucrative concerts and record dates he'd have to cancel to come back from California; $1,500 is cheap. As Sophie Tucker said, "I've been rich and I've been poor . . . rich is better."

I was tempted to take the same route when the prosecution

suggested we plead guilty to breach of peace, pay a twenty-five-dollar fine and the other charges would be dropped. But the legal lawyers, as Lindy Stokes calls them, decided that a unilateral action like this on my part would damage Robin and Bruno; they offered to pay for my case also. Thanks to *Life Magazine*'s money, I was still not guilty in the eyes of the law. Did you hear that, Sophie?

And how, rich is better! If you make, say, a hundred dollars a week and are supporting a wife and a few kids, you won't qualify for legal aid because you're not quite destitute. But neither can you afford the time and expense of a defense; you lose, guilty or not. The odds are with pleading guilty in front. There's only one drawback: a police record.

So, two weeks later, we were up at six-thirty again, on the turnpike by seven-thirty, in the lawyer's office by nine and in court by ten. Our witnesses were there: Fred Powledge, another writer for *Life,* Steve Burbank, a senior at Harvard who had observed our busts and volunteered his name and address to Fred, plus a few character witnesses.

Accused come out of a padlocked door, some go back in, others are suspended; everything is processed, documents shifted from one pile to another, cases come and go. Nothing is solved. Set bails, change pleas—recess. Wait and smoke outside. Some continuances. Lunch. Wait. Smoke. At two o'clock, case number sixty your honor: Sam Thompson. Is Sam Thompson in the court? Sam Thompson steps forward in need of a shave. His legal aid pleads extenuating circumstances and the judge pins thirty days on Sam, suspending it.

Another judge this time: Judge Rottman. Must I describe him? He looks just like his name. Our case was finally called; but no, patrolman Grandly had phoned in sick with laryngitis and, without its star witness, the state wanted a continuance. Our lawyer pleaded extreme inconvenience: "Your

Honor, these people are from out of town." He requested that the charges be dropped.

His Honor stared, bored, and denied. A new date was set two weeks later, at which time we went through the same thing all over again without Bruno. On assignment somewhere, he had left instructions to forfeit his bail. The power of the state was beginning to tell; we were suffering casualties.

The prosecution kept the initiative, refusing to try us without Bruno, on the technicality that our lawyer had not formally moved to separate the cases. The judge agreed that to try us without him would be an "undue hardship on the state."

Judge Rottman was a pillar, his face a study of the fix. Not a pay-off or graft or anything simple like that—a total fix: accepted, permanent, legal, and hopeless. "Give me your tired, your poor, your huddled masses yearning to breathe free, the wretched refuse of your teeming shore, send these, the homeless, the tempest-tost to me . . ." and fuck all of you forever.

This case was a real nuisance. No prosecutor or judge wanted it. Any technicality on which to base a postponement was seized on. Under normal circumstances, people like us would have made our deal and quit long ago. We were, according to our lawyer, a rather special case.

The fourth time the trial could no longer be avoided. The same courtroom scene this time, only the judge had changed and, it was apparent from the beginning, for the better.

Judge Philip Dwyer could play Joseph Welch in "the Joe McCarthy Story." Extremely short, bald with a small grey fringe and a pixyish smile, his clip-on bow tie completes the picture. Handling the morning casting session, he was always ready to smile and he acted with about as much compassion as the script allows.

The prosecutor, Herb Scott, is a busy man who must keep the action moving at all costs. We had had many rehearsals;

our witnesses were substantial people, lucid and sure of their veracity. All Herb Scott had was patrolman Grandly, a shifty witness who did not tell the truth, although I couldn't say whether he was lying or forgetful.

In any case, the tables had turned. The trial, which lasted four hours, was worthy of Perry Mason. Witnesses were cross-examined, Bruno's photos were introduced as evidence, objections were allowed and overruled. Judge Dwyer took notes diligently, ruling carefully and asking many questions.

Grandly said I had interfered along with Bruno and that we had been arrested together. He related how Robin had leaped on his back and scratched his neck. Our witnesses testified otherwise. Summing up, our lawyer pointed out that patrolman Grandly had been wearing an overcoat, the collar of which covered his neck. The witnesses had testified that it was impossible for Bruno and I to have been arrested at the same time. Our case looked like a lead-pipe cinch.

Judge Dwyer retired to chambers to study his thick sheaf of notes, remaining there fifteen minutes. Resettled on the bench, he gave his opinion: a monument to lucidity, logic, and the law. He spoke quietly, formal but not without humor, and the courtroom no longer seemed so dismal.

He dismissed the charges one by one until only interfering with a police officer remained against Robin. Carefully considering his words, he said: "I suppose, technically, she could be found guilty of interfering. She did hold up an officer in his duty of executing an arrest and removing the accused expeditiously from the scene so that the arrest would not prompt more trouble. But I think it was an impetuous act and she did not intend to interfere. I see no purpose being served in finding her guilty. We certainly don't need her money and the fine would be nominal in any case. She is only twenty-four, next year she will be twenty-five, some day she will be fifty and possibly look back on all of this with some degree of humor . . . and I imagine she has learned a lesson already. I find her not guilty."

All the way he was careful with Grandly, complimenting him whenever possible and stating he was not implying that the officer had lied, only that the state had not proved its case beyond any reasonable doubt, which is its obligation.

Judge Dwyer stopped to chat with us in the hall. He had enjoyed this case, he said. "All morning, during the usual hubbub, I was thinking of my afternoon with the Ivy League."

Nothing had changed, I realized. We had been acquitted not so much from innocence, but because our economic position had permitted us the luxury of seeing the case through to trial.

I thought of Ike, Bill, Wally, Rocky, and the others at ARC trying to make out in so-called normal society after a lifetime of running from it. What chance would they have under false arrest? They would probably have wound up in jail. Could I stand so-called normal society, sober in Harlem?

Leaving after my most recent visit to the Center, I passed Flagg on the stoop. Anna Kosof told me later how he'd begged to be readmitted. This time he meant business, he said. The staff still had the matter under consideration. What will happen to Flagg? Either way, he will still be lost in the "hubbub of the morning."

I cannot forget Judge Rottman's face, or the expression on Grandly's as we were acquitted. We got away with something only because we were "them." Next time Grandly will be more careful who he roughs up—and will probably be even rougher.

As long as we accept our streets as they are and leave patrolman Grandly in charge of them, we will remain with only neighborhoods. Until all children grow up in communities fit to live in, until big money can't buy justice, until the "squares" who run the world become "hip," there will be ever more active dope fiends; no matter how many James Allens come along.

This is not a happy ending.